The
NON-ALCOHOLIC
Pocket
Bartender's Guide
by Jill Cox

A Fireside Book
Published by Simon & Schuster Inc.
New York London Toronto Sydney Tokyo

The Nonalcoholic Pocket Bartender's Guide
Edited and designed by
Mitchell Beazley International Limited
Artists House, 14–15 Manette Street, London
W1V 5LB
Copyright © Mitchell Beazley Publishers 1988
Text copyright © Jill Cox 1988
Photographs and illustrations copyright © Mitchell
Beazley Publishers 1988

A FIRESIDE BOOK
Published by Simon & Schuster Inc.
Simon & Schuster Building
Rockefeller Center
1230 Avenue of the Americas
New York, New York 10020

FIRESIDE and colophon are registered trademarks
of Simon & Schuster Inc.

ISBN 0-671-67343-2

10 9 8 7 6 5 4 3 2

First published in 1988 in Great Britain by Mitchell
Beazley Publishers, London.
The author and publishers will be grateful for any
information which will assist them in keeping future
editions up to date. Although all reasonable care
has been taken in the preparation of this
book neither the publishers nor the author can accept any
liability for any consequences arising from the use
thereof or from the information contained herein.

Acknowledgements
With grateful thanks to Alison Grainge and Wendy Lee for
their invaluable help and enthusiasm.

Editor Alison Melvin
Art Editor Paul Drayson
Senior Executive Editor Chris Foulkes
Senior Executive Art Editor Roger Walton
Production Stewart Bowling
Illustrations by Allan Drummond
Photography by Sally Cushing
Typeset by Bookworm Typesetting, Manchester,
England.
Produced by Mandarin Offset
Printed in Shekou, China

CONTENTS

CONTENTS

INTRODUCTION

This is a book about enjoying a drink without drinking alcohol. It is addressed to those who have decided not to drink alcohol – for health or other reasons – and to those who feel that their well-being gains from occasional abstinence. There is a place in everyone's life for a repertoire of attractive, flavorful and sophisticated non-alcoholic drinks. Perhaps the best reason of all for turning to non-alcoholic drinks is because we want to try new, exciting tastes, to tempt our own and our friends' palates with something they've never experienced before.

The book is also a celebration of a neglected range of taste sensations. Drinks which contain no alcohol have been neglected as all the critical attention has been directed at wines, beers and spirits together with the various mixed drinks made from them. The aim is to show that no alcohol doesn't mean no fun, no taste and no refreshment. The reverse is true: non-alcoholic drinks can be as exotic, as flavorsome and at least as refreshing as anything based on alcohol. The recent wave of mineral waters and de-alcoholized drinks are signs that people want alternatives to alcohol.

Many of the earth's cultures have always managed without alcohol (though they tend to have other stimulants). Traditional drinks from these regions are the inspiration for some recipes, while others come from country communities in our own part of the world. More use the widening range of exotic fruits and vegetables available in our markets and stores.

Even the alcoholic drinks industry is coming to terms with the new desire for healthy drinking. Responding to public tastes, drinks companies are marketing a range of low-alcohol coolers and other wine-based drinks. Exciting progress is being made with non-alcoholic wines and beers, which now taste virtually like the 'real' thing. But beware: even those drinks marketed as 'alcohol free' sometimes have traces of alcohol in them. Alcohol is a natural product, the result of a very basic chemical reaction. As such it occurs in products such as fruit juices which we do not think of as 'alcoholic'. If it is important to you to totally avoid alcohol, take a careful look at bottle labels. In this book, drinks which have traces of alcohol are marked with a special symbol ✿ (see How To Use p. 33).

The 200 original recipes in this book have been devised to provide a selection of exciting, colorful, exotic and sensuous, fruity, refreshing and comforting drinks. Drinks based on citrus fruits and berries will appeal to all age groups. Fizzes of every flavor and shade refresh and quench thirst. Sultry chocolate and coffee drinks made sometimes with milk, cream or yogurt are luxurious treats. Exotic and spicy recipes using tropical fruits and fresh spices, or infusions of teas and herbs for delicious refreshers and punches, are aromatic and unusual. And super summer slushes made from crushed ice and sorbets are perfect summer coolers.

Most importantly, there's a great choice of drinks you may have never even considered which could become part of your regular diet. Vegetable drinks, for example, are rich in vitamins and minerals and served chilled are a stimulating savory aperitif.

The first, and most obvious, non-alcoholic drink is – water. Today, there is more to water than what comes out of a tap. So we survey the world of bottled waters, which offers a wide variety of refreshment and a contribution to healthy living.

Non-alcoholic drinks offer opportunities to tempt other senses besides the palate. The section on garnishes, preparation and decoration offers hints on making the drinks even more attractive to the eye. It's followed by a color-illustrated chapter on serving suggestions which shows how attractive the drinks can look. And the main section of the book comprises recipes for every kind of non-alcoholic drink. So if you fancy something a little different, a drink which tastes great, looks good and is alcohol-free – read on.

CHAPTER 1

THE WATER WAVE

The average person needs about a liter of liquid a day to survive. Water is the obvious, and sometimes the only answer. It's usually freely and widely available, and as a result is often taken for granted.

The serious commercial water business seems to have started in Europe at a time when local water supplies were undrinkable. Today, France leads the world in consumption with 70 liters per annum for every person in the land. Bottled water of the still and carbonated varieties is part of the culture.

In recent years in other parts of the world, a new generation has emerged that steadfastly refuses to swallow water from a tap, even though it is perfectly safe to do so. Instead, their water has to be packaged. This is good news for those with a natural spring in the back garden and the glass and aluminium industries that supply the bottles and cans. But is there any justification for such action? It appears not. Numerous tests by guardians of local community water supplies across the western world reveal that there is little discernible difference between water drawn from the local reservoir, and the packaged water of branded water suppliers.

Facts probably influence consumers less than fashions, however. And among the weight-conscious and the health-conscious, mineral waters are very firmly in fashion, cleverly promoted as they are by suppliers whose profit margins can finance big spends on advertising.

The issues of health and curative powers of natural water have in fact been attracting the landed gentry to Europe's natural springs for centuries. The pretty Belgian town of Spa was among the first to make a name for itself as a popular watering hole with its mineral waters gushing from deep in the Ardennes. It seems likely that the name became synonomous with waters believed to have medicinal properties. As a result a number of English towns and cities that had the good fortune to boast a local supply of natural mineral water adopted the term. So places like Bath, Harrogate and Leamington Spa are historical old medicinal water towns.

Each of these spas claimed benefits for certain disorders. The water from Harrogate in the north of

England for example was thought to be good for scurvy and syphilis, while Leamington water took care of erruptions about the face. Taking the waters not only meant swallowing the odd glass or two but also bodily immersion. The ultimate curative powers claimed by water are of course at Lourdes in France.

It is of course the minute quantities of minerals and salts that make water from one source taste different from another. And whilst in earlier times good medicine equated to a nasty taste, these days, waters that are low in salt are heralded as being the most desirable and beneficial. Most of the best known waters literally spring from vast underground lakes after being filtered naturally through porous rocks formed millions of years ago. Such conditions ensure purity but to be safe, pollution conscious nations throughout the world have begun to lay down strict rules relating to the quality of mineral waters and their sources. Europe, home of the most famous names in the water business, maintains that its water products must come from an underground as opposed to surface lake; they must contain no bacteria; be bottled at source and contain mineral traces at specified levels. There is a considerable difference in salt content between the various brands of mineral water. Indeed were there not, then a panel of expert wine tasters gathered in London for a tasting of various waters would have found their task impossible.

Vichy and Apollinaris are reckoned to have a salty taste while the more popular Perrier and Badoit brands score on their brisk bubbles. It is in fact the bubbles that attract most drinkers. Outside France three-quarters of all mineral water sold is carbonated.

Twenty years ago the art was to appear to be drinking hard liquor by merely drinking tonic water, today it is positively chic to be seen clutching a glass of crystal clear fizzy water.

CHAPTER 2

WHO'S WHO IN MINERAL WATER

FRANCE

Most mineral water rises from natural underground supplies in mountainous regions such as the Massif Central, the Alps and the Vosges. It often picks up trace elements and minerals from the rocks, and can be naturally sparkling due to gases within it.

BADOIT springs from an underground lake at Saint-Galmier, 500 metres below the granite Monts de Lyonnais in the Massif Central in the Loire region of central France. It emerges lightly carbonated, with a degree of fluoride. First bottled over 150 years ago, Badoit has digestive qualities which aid the gastric process.

CONTREXEVILLE water filters through a strata of limestone in the Vosges Mountains for two years before arriving at a vast underground lake. The resulting still water is high in mineral salts and is often drunk for its curative and diuretic properties. Not as well-known as other French waters.

EVIAN still water flows from a spring near Evian on the lake of Geneva, Lac Léman. It has a low mineral content and because of its purity is greatly favored as everyday drinking water. Evian is pure because it takes an estimated 15 years for the Alpine snow to filter through the hillsides to collect in a deep sand-based reservoir protected by two thick layers of clay. The water has been available in Paris and other European capitals since the 1850s and has been exported to North America since the turn of the century

PERRIER, the worldwide leading brand of naturally sparkling water, comes from Vergeze, on the Languedoc Plain in the south of France. An Englishman, St John Harmsworth, named the water after a Dr Perrier who introduced him to the spring in 1903. Stimulating and refreshing, the water has large enthusiastic bubbles and a discreet mineral taste. The distinctive, green, tear-shaped bottle is based on the Indian clubs Harmsworth used to exercise with whilst recovering from a car accident. Available in liter or 25cl bottles. Range includes lemon and lime flavored varieties. Large advertising spends over a number of years have enabled the brand name to become almost a generic term for sparkling mineral water.

VICHY CELESTINS is a naturally carbonated mineral water, high in mineral content. A visit to the town, located to the west of Lyon in the centre of France, to take the waters has been a well-established practice since Napoleonic times. Vichy offers a distinctive rather salty taste that has its origins in a high content of bicarbonate of soda.

VITTEL still water, sold in square plastic bottles, is from the Vosges mountains in eastern France. There are two varieties, a medium mineralisation version Vittel Grande Source or Vittel Hepar which has a higher mineral content.

VOLVIC is a pure, light, still mountain water from the volcanic highlands of the Auvergne in central France. It has a low sodium and calcium content with some magnesium, which makes it suitable for those on low salt diets. The waters spring from a huge natural filter in a shallow dip between volcanic hills after draining for many years through porous basalt rocks onto a granite base.

ITALY

FERRARELLE Originates north-east of Naples near an extinct volcano. This water is naturally sparkling from carbon dioxide found in the volcanic sub-strata. The Romans liked it because it mixed well with wine. Rich in calcium and bicarbonates, it aids digestion, too.

SAN PELLEGRINO Italy's best known mineral water was established in 1899. Bottled at source, the water has been shipped to the United States for decades. The water comes from three springs at the foothills of the Italian Alps just north-east of Milan. Leonardo da Vinci is alleged to have drunk it. An alkaline water, the local village people and visitors drink it as it emerges from underground as a still water from five public fountains. It tastes of minerals, but much of this is lost in the processes of carbonation. The resulting water is a fresh and frisky, flavorful quencher.

BELGIUM

SPA Around for 400 years, this water is available still or sparkling. Spa is a term now synonymous with natural mineral springs, but it was originally the name of a small town in the Ardennes in Belgium. Low in mineral salts, the sparkling variety has vigorous busy bubbles and a clean fresh taste.

WEST GERMANY

APPOLLINARIS Germany's favorite sparkling water from the Ahr valley. High in carbonation, this is refreshing and effervescent with a distinct taste from the high mineral content – a natural blend of calcium, magnesium, potassium and sodium which makes it an excellent digestive.

SWEDEN

RAMLOSA A natural mineral water drawn from the underground spring in Ramlosa, outside Helsingborg in the south of Sweden. This is a softly sparkling water with gently rambling bubbles and silky feel on the tongue. Find it in a distinctive ice-blue bottle with a neck wide enough to drink from.

ENGLAND

MALVERN Considered to be the best mixer with whisky due to its purity and low mineral content. This simple water which springs from the granite Malvern Hills in the west of England has been highly thought of since the 1600s. It occurs naturally as a still water but a carbonated Malvern has been available since the 1980s. The English royal family takes it abroad with them to avoid drinking suspect local water.

USA

MOUNTAIN VALLEY The best-known natural spring water in the United States which comes from Hot Springs, Arkansas is still, low in salt and mildly alkaline. Fans of Mountain Valley include Frank Sinatra, Mick Jagger and Mohammed Ali. It has been the water of the White House since Coolidge was president.

CHAPTER 3

THE FINAL TOUCH

An enticing glass of refreshment is even more attractive with a little subtle decoration. Ideally this should be relevant to the drink and not simply a slice or sprig of anything you happen to have.

Garnishes can range from a single stuffed olive or cocktail cherry to herbs, curls of citrus peel, fancy ice cubes colored with juice, or containing tiny edible flowers, sprinklings of finely chopped nuts, freshly ground spices or grated chocolate – depending on the drink. Suggestions for appropriate garnishes are given with each recipe. Experiment yourself, too and try some of the fancy decorations below.

ICE

Just about the most important ingredient in a non-alcoholic drink – the clinking in the glass makes it SOUND right. If you think your tap water leaves something to be desired, use still bottled water or boiled, cooled tap water for good taste. But ice doesn't have to be just ice. And it isn't always cubes. Today's ice trays freeze cubes, balls, little cones and endless other icy shapes to chill drinks. And it's amazing what you can freeze into shapes of ice to make them pretty. Mint leaves, tiny wedges of lime, lemon or orange, even flowers, make attractive and unusual decorations.

You can make fruit juice cubes to add flavor and color to chilled drinks but these melt very quickly. Add a dash of vegetable coloring for tinted ice cubes; blue and green cubes are rather exotic. Frozen coffee ice cubes are a chic way of cooling iced coffee. Vegetable juices freeze, too. And it's possible to freeze herbal infusions to add to vegetable cocktails, but they are usually a subtle shade of green, so be careful to match to the drink.

CRUSHED ICE Some cocktails are better when poured over crushed ice. These are usually strongly flavored drinks, as the ice melts quickly to dilute the drink. To make crushed ice, whiz a dozen ice cubes in a food processor using the metal blade. Do this at the last minute and use immediately. If you don't have a processor freeze a block of ice in a cube tray with the grid removed. Take out the block, wrap it in a cloth and hit it with a wooden rolling pin or mallet until it is crushed enough. Do not use a blender for crushing ice as you are likely to break the blade.

ICE BLOCKS For punches you need a block of ice to keep the punch bowl cool – a block will melt more slowly than cubes. To make, simply remove the grid from ice cube tray and freeze.

FROSTED GLASSES

SWEET AND SAVORY FROSTING Sparkly, crystal edging to glasses is attractive for both sweet (use sugar), and savory (use sparing salt) cocktails. Sprinkle sugar or salt on a saucer. Invert glass into a saucer of lemon juice, or rub a slice of lemon around the rim, squeezing enough to moisten the top of the glass. Dip edge into sugar or salt and crystals will set in a frosty rim.

COLORED FROSTING Drinks using colored syrup can be frosted to match the syrup. Dip rim of glass in syrup, then into the sugar.

FLAVORED FROSTING Nutty drinks can be served in glasses with the rims dipped in lemon juice, and then into finely chopped almonds, or coconut – to match the drink.

FRUIT DECORATIONS

LEMON, LIME AND ORANGE Use to decorate the edge of the glass. Cut a thin slice from the middle of the lemon and try to avoid the seeds. Make another cut from the peel to the center of the slice. Hook slice over rim of glass. Use mixed slices for a pretty and colorful multi-garnish, spiked on a cocktail stick.

TWISTS Twist the cut fruit slice around in opposite directions and secure with a cocktail stick. Rest on edge of glass.

TWIRLS Thinly pare a spiral of zest from entire fruit using a potato peeler, taking care not to include any pith. It will curl on its own. Use to twirl down over the outside of the glass hooking the top curl on to the rim.

PEACHES AND APRICOTS Cut thin slices from fresh fruit – never use canned, the sugar in the syrup will upset the balance of the drink. Spear on a cocktail stick and rest on the rim of the glass.

MELON Scoop into balls, or cut into small dice if you don't have a balling gadget. Use a variety of different melons for punches to give different colored balls. Water melon is pink, Honeydew yellow and Ogen orange. Float on top of drinks. Or spike three different colored balls on a cocktail stick and rest on the edge of the glass.

APPLES AND PEARS Choose unblemished fruit with brightly colored skins. Core and quarter fruit, then cut into thin slices. Dip briefly in lemon juice and use as a garnish on cocktail sticks or to float on top of drinks.

BERRIES Whole strawberries, raspberries, blackberries and loganberries make pretty garnishes, either whole or halved vertically. Wash, and dry, leaving the leaf intact if it has one, and float on top of drink. Drape small bunches of black currants, red currants or white currants over the edge of glasses. Currants freeze well and can be kept for future use.

CHERRIES Cherries were invented for garnishing. Twos and threes hook automatically over the edge of a glass. Freeze in ice cubes for a glamorous clink, or use in a fruity punch as a bobbing up and down decoration. Cocktail cherries are available in yellow, green, blue and purple varieties as well as red. Always spear on a cocktail stick before using as a decoration. Frost fresh, pitted cherries by dipping in egg white then into superfine sugar, for a sparkly garnish.

PINEAPPLE Leave the skin on and cut thin slices of pineapple horizontally, then slice into triangular wedges. Float on drinks, or spear on cocktail sticks. Make a cut from the pointed end to within ½in (1cm) of the skin and rest over the edge of the glass.

GRAPES Use seedless grapes for scattering on top of punches, or small bunches for decorating individual glasses. Spike a few on a cocktail stick with pitted cherries for a sophisticated garnish.

EXOTIC Cut kiwifruit and starfruit in horizontal

slices for an exotic and unusual decoration, especially for fruit punches. Peel the kiwifruit and leave the skin on the starfruit. Peel fresh, pitted lychees. Spike on a cocktail stick and balance on glass.

VEGETABLES

CELERY AND SPRING ONIONS Celery sticks cut thinly make stirrers you can leave in the drink as a garnish, preferably with a bit of feathery leaf left on. So do tasseled spring onions. To make these, trim onions, then make thin, 1in (2cm) vertical cuts down the green end of each onion. Leave in iced water and green ends will twizzle into a tassle.

CUCUMBER Use cucumber slices as a garnish. Leave skin on. Or score with a canelle gadget to make stripy grooves down the length of the cucumber to give slices with decorative "notches". Long sticks of cucumber also make good vegetable cocktail stirrers. Balls of cucumber are attractive, too. Scoop out with a melon baller. Leave to drain before using.

CARROTS AND COURGETTES Peel long, thin carrots or courgettes. Using a potato peeler pare off thin "ribbons". Soak for an hour in iced water and they will curl up to make a pretty and crunchy vegetable garnish.

SKEWERS Make little skewers consisting of cocktail onions and black or green olives to rest on the top of vegetable cocktails. Or assemble baby kebabs with slices of carrot, gherkin, shallot and green, red and yellow peppers.

HERBS

Always use fresh herbs. Mint sprigs or leaves are bold, erect and fragrant. Marjoram is frond-like, and hangs down over the edge of the glass. But try any herb as a garnish for herbal or savory drinks. Basil, parsley, borage, coriander and even a little twig of rosemary add scent and a touch of style.

FLOWERS

Edible flowers, or their petals make a pretty and unusual decoration — both sprinkled on the top of a drink or punch, or frozen inside ice cubes. Rose and

marigold petals, honeysuckle, nasturtium and prim-
rose flowers are suitable, and there are dozens
more. Be sure to check that flowers are edible.

NUTS

Finely chopped almonds, walnuts, or coconut can
be used to edge glasses, dipped in lemon juice, or
egg white. You can also use chopped nuts as a
garnish on chocolate, coffee, or malty drinks, or milk
shakes. For a special decoration for exotic drinks,
pare fresh coconut with a potato peeler, then lightly
toast to a gentle pale brown for a curly, nutty twizzle.

SPICES

Powdered spices like cloves, or cinnamon are good
on milk, yogurt, malty, chocolate or coffee drinks for
a subtle addition of flavor. Always use freshly-
grated nutmeg for the best taste. And go easy, you
only need a sprinkling of any of these spices.
Cinnamon sticks make pretty stirrers.

GINGER

Preserved stem ginger finely chopped is an exotic
and unexpected garnish. Use the syrup in the
cocktail and a cocktail stick threaded with thin slices
of preserved stem ginger as a garnish.

CHOCOLATE

Chocolate curls made on the medium holes of the
grater make super, curly decorations. Use milk,
plain, or white chocolate.
   For a really sophisticated garnish make curls of
chocolate caraque in advance. Melt chocolate and
spread over a worktop thinly. Leave until just set.
Holding a sharp chopping knife at an angle of 45
degrees, scrape the blade across the set chocolate
so a thin layer curls up under the blade into a wafer
thin cigarillo. Decorate after dinner chocolate or
coffee drinks with this.

SYRUP

Bright syrups like strawberry and black currant can
be used to drizzle on top of ice cream, cream
topped cocktails, or milk shakes for the final touch.

CHAPTER 4

SERVING SUGGESTIONS

The following 16 pages of photographs illustrate a selection of the non-alcoholic drinks featured in this book. Displayed to their best advantage in full-color, they show the amazing variety of colors, textures and effects that can be obtained by following the recipes and hints for serving. The pages featuring ingredients and garnishes in particular should get your taste buds and imagination working and inspire you to try these soft drinks for yourself or dream up some of your own recipes.

Below left to right: Emerald (p.100); Sunriser (p.39); Dream Machine (p.41); Pillar-Box (p.71).

PICK OF THE CROP

Shown on these two pages are just some of the delicious ingredients which form the basis for these recipes. They range from fresh fruit and vegetables, milk and yogurt to exotic spices and herbs – the variety is endless.

Only ingredients that are readily available have been featured in the book, but do remember that fresh produce is seasonal and may be more expensive at certain times of the year.

Often, however, a substitute can be found to give an alcohol-free cocktail with an individual touch – don't be afraid to experiment. The freshness of fruit and vegetables is not essential if it is only used for squeezing juice or extracting flavor, but care should be taken not to use under- or over-ripe produce. For garnishes and fruit punches, where looks are all important, the very best quality available is a must.

TASTE OF SUMMER

Pictured below are some of the fruit-based drinks featured in the recipes. Making use of freshly squeezed juices, these drinks not only look good, they are also packed with vitamins and minerals and will do you good too. Fruit syrups are high

LAVA FLOW (P.35) ▶

◀ ENGLISH SUMMER (P.38)

BILLY BUNTER (P.40) ▶

in sugar so they should only be used in small quantities. They are especially useful for giving pretty graded stripes to drinks – the heavier syrups sink to the bottom of the glass.

SWEET AND SOUR (P.47) ▶

◀ MAGIC MOUNTAIN (P.38)

RUNNING SHORTS (P.45) ▶

PARTY PUNCHES

Stunning festive and fun party punches
for help yourself, sip and come again imbibers.
These are colorful and refreshing quenchers
suitable for every kind of occasion and for every
age group. They are ideal for children's parties, and
so much healthier than fizzy drinks with
additives and colorings.
Planning a summer picnic? Then why not make up
one of the recipes the night before, such as
Citrus Barley Water, and put it into a vacuum flask

with plenty of ice for a sophisticated and refreshing reviver. Try the Spiced Ale Punch on a cold winter night or for an alcohol-free approach to Christmas or New Year festivities.

Pictured below in the glass punch bowl on the left hand page is Country Garden (p.130). On the right hand page in the single glass is Shamgria (p.131) and Melodramatic Punch (p.127) is the drink served in the melon shell.

There's a drink here for every occasion – whether it's a celebration or simply a refreshing drink to quench your thirst. Pina Colada is a delicious alcohol-free party drink; Flamingo Flame and Pep Up are just right for sipping on a hot summer day; Aztec King

◀ PINA COLADA (P.50)

FLAMINGO FLAME (P.67) ▶

◀ AZTEC KING (P.74)

makes a tasty aperitif and refreshers like Tutti Frutti and Court Jester need no excuses for drinking. You might even say these drinks are an occasion in themselves with their vibrant colors and deliciously unusual flavors.

◀ PEP UP (P.62)

TUTTI FRUTTI (P.105) ▶

◀ COURT JESTER (P.102)

SLIMLINERS

Although no drink has fewer calories than a glass of plain water, you may want to sample something with a bit more taste but still containing fewer calories than most soft (or hard) drinks. Of course, these drinks will also appeal to all those concerned with maintaining a healthy diet. Most of the other recipes can also be adapted for a lower calorie count by substituting skimmed milk or leaving out any sugar or honey.

Pictured below from left to right: Slim Line (p.106); Milord (p.107); Slinky (p.106).

AFTER DARK

As a complete contrast to the slimliner drinks, most
of these are *not* recommended for anyone who is
limiting their calorie intake. Chocolate drinks
enriched with cream, ice cream or mint syrup are
pure indulgences and delicious as after-dinner
treats or even instead of dessert. Coffee and tea
cocktails are either cooling refreshers or sensuous
luxuries. Sophisticated tea drinks have fabulous
flavors and fragrances and are especially refreshing
on balmy summer evenings.

Pictured below from left to right:
The Waldorf (p.114); Beverley Hills (p.85);
Minte Carlo (p.88); Chocablok (p.90).

FRESH FROM THE COUNTRY

Healthy and pure vegetable juices are delicious on
their own – or as a base for mixed vegetable drinks.
They range from freshly squeezed juices of carrot or
cucumber to thick purées of avocado blended with
honey. Herbal drinks are scented and transparent
infusions. Make an infusion by covering the herb
with hot or boiling water to extract the most flavor.

Pictured below from left to right: Carrot Juice (p.72);
Cold Curer (p.80); Healthy Cooler (p.74).

TROPICAL DELIGHTS

Tropical fruits from all over the world are the starting
point for a wide variety of rich tasting and exciting
fruit cocktails and punches. For an extra kick some
are pepped up with spices, or sharpened with lime
juice. Mangoes, papayas, passion fruit and guavas
are now everyday food items in supermarkets and
can be used for colorful drinks with distinctive flavors
and heady perfumes. Try using some of the more
unfamiliar exotic fruits available. Starfruit, for
example, makes a stunning garnish to a fruit punch.

Pictured below from left to right: Almond Grove
(p.96); Tango in the Night (p.95).

THE FINAL TOUCH

Chocolate curls, toasted coconut and walnuts are some ideas for decorating rich chocolate and coffee drinks.

Ice cubes are one of the most important ingredients. Freeze fruit in ice and serve with long drinks.

Fruit slices can be cut and twisted into a variety of shapes for decoration of all fruit based drinks.

Ribbons and slices of attractively cut fresh vegetables make an edible addition to vegetable juices.

Y Cocktail Glass
Exotic, sophisticated
tastes. Also used for
glamorous concoctions.

Y Tall Glass
Suitable for long, thirst
quenching fruit drinks,
or fizzy soda drinks.

Y Short Glass
Rich tasting drinks
with distinctive tastes
and textures.

Y Wine Glass
Sip and come again
drinks. Useful for
punches.

▪ Chunky Glass
A meal in a glass. For
strongly flavored and
thick vegetable drinks.

▶ Heatproof Glass
Essential for all hot and
spicy punches. Also for
some herbal infusions.

CHAPTER 5

How To Use This Book

The following cocktail recipes are arranged under headings according to their main ingredient. To find drinks that contain a specific ingredient, consult the ingredient index on pp. 133-136.

To make them easy to follow, most of the recipes have been written using a "parts" system when it is not absolutely necessary to have an exact measurement. For example, one part of one ingredient and one of another served in a tall glass means they are included in equal quantities to fill that glass. The size of glass is indicated by the glass symbol (opposite). However, these are only suggestions and the drinks will taste just as good in whatever type of glass you choose to serve them in. Each recipe is designed for one person, unless a volume quantity is specified above the list of ingredients. Making drinks in larger quantities is simply a matter of increasing the ingredients in proportion to the number of drinkers.

The introduction to each recipe describes the taste, color and texture of the drink. The glass symbol will also give an indication of the kind of drink it is.

Mid-Atlantic terms are used for certain ingredients in order that the recipes can be easily followed by readers in the United States and Europe. Measurements where necessary are given with metric and American alternatives.

It should be pointed out that some recipes (particularly the party punches) include de-alcoholized products like wines, or bitters. Both of these contain a trace of alcohol. These recipes have the ✳ symbol to indicate they are not *totally* alcohol-free and not suitable for those readers who *must* avoid alcohol even in very small amounts.

CHAPTER 6

FRUIT COCKTAILS

Citrus fruits, berries and other fruits form the base of these drinks. Some are long and refreshing, others are rich and fruity. Plus there's a home-made lemon cordial for diluting with lots of ice for lazy weekends. And a few sophisticated cocktails, too.

RED DEVIL

Strawberry fruitiness with the fullness of oranges for a delectable summer freshener.

---

4 STRAWBERRIES, WIPED AND HULLED

JUICE OF ½ ORANGE

TOP UP WITH SODA WATER

Whiz up all ingredients in a blender. Pour into a glass and serve chilled. 🍷

BLACK PRINCE

Bittersweet black currant sundowner.

---

1 PART PINEAPPLE JUICE

1 PART GRAPEFRUIT JUICE

2 TBSP BLACK CURRANT SYRUP

Mix juices together in a glass. Drizzle in syrup to make a purple layer on the bottom. ▼

LAVA FLOW

Surprisingly the egg yolk in this mixes with the citrus juices to give a rich, smooth and creamy but refreshing drink.

---

2 PARTS ORANGE JUICE

JUICE OF ½ LEMON

1 TBSP BOTTLED SWEETENED LIME JUICE

1 EGG YOLK, BROKEN UP WITH A FORK

1 PART SPARKLING MINERAL WATER

2 ICE CUBES

SLICE OF LEMON, LIME AND ORANGE

Shake orange juice, fresh lemon juice, lime and egg yolk in a container with a tight fitting lid – a cocktail shaker will do, until it is a golden color with a smooth and sensuous texture. Top up with mineral water to taste. Put ice into a processor and whiz for about six seconds, to make crushed ice. Spoon into the bottom of a glass and pour drink over. Decorate with fruit slices. ▼

Unless stated, serve cocktails in chilled glasses. Chill in the fridge for an hour.

BLACK CURRANT BREW

Unusual and daintily flavored black currant refresher, packed with vitamin C.

2 TBSP FRESH BLACK CURRANTS

1 PART PLAIN YOGURT

1 PART MILK, CHILLED

2 TBSP BLACK CURRANT SYRUP

FEW BLACK CURRANTS AND LEAVES TO DECORATE

Pick over black currants and remove stalks. Wash and dry fruit. Whiz up all ingredients in a blender until it looks a smooth, pale purple color. Pour into a glass and decorate with black currants. ▼

LEMON SYRUP

A luscious lemon cordial for diluting with water to taste. Makes 1 liter.

2 JUICY LEMONS, WASHED

700G (3 CUPS) SUGAR

600ML (2½ CUPS) WATER

Thinly pare rinds from lemons. Add to sugar and pour over water in a pan. Bring to the boil and simmer for 10 minutes. Cool. Squeeze juice of lemons and add to water syrup. Strain and bottle. To use, pour into a glass and dilute to taste. ▼

HURRICANE FORCE

Champagne-colored drink with
pineapple floaters. Refreshing quencher
with fast, busy bubbles.

½ PART CRUSHED PINEAPPLE

---

1 PART APPLE JUICE

---

1 PART TONIC WATER

Spoon pineapple into bottom of a glass. Top up with
apple juice and tonic water for a refreshing fizz. ▪

IN THE PINK

Refreshing citrus blush.

JUICE OF 1 PINK GRAPEFRUIT

150ML (⅔ CUP) ORANGE JUICE

---

2 TBSP SUGAR

TOP UP WITH SODA WATER

Put grapefruit and orange juice in a glass. Sprinkle in
sugar and chill for one hour. Top up with soda. ▼

CHARIOTS OF FIRE

Blazing flame-colored drink with a touch
of gingery spice.

---

1 PART ORANGE JUICE

---

1 PART GINGER ALE

Pour into a glass and mix with a cocktail stirrer. ▼

MAGIC MOUNTAIN

Frothy, purple blackberry refresher.

2 TBSP BLACKBERRIES

1 TBSP MAPLE SYRUP

300ML (1 ¼ CUPS) APPLE JUICE

FRESH BLACKBERRY TO DECORATE

Whiz up all ingredients in a blender. Pour into a glass and decorate with a fresh blackberry. ▼

ENGLISH SUMMER

Strawberry-pink with delicate fruit, a hint of mint and a kick of lemon. Sparkles up when the soda is added.

1 PART FRESHLY SQUEEZED LEMON JUICE

1 PART STRAWBERRY SYRUP

SPRIG OF FRESH MINT

TOP UP WITH SODA WATER

2 ICE CUBES

PINK COCKTAIL UMBRELLA

FRESH STAWBERRY, HULLED AND WIPED

FEW FRESH MINT LEAVES

Pour lemon juice into a glass and add syrup. Finely chop mint and sprinkle over. Top up with soda and add ice cubes. Thread strawberry onto cocktail umbrella with mint leaves for decoration. ▼

SUNRISER

Two-tone pink and orange sunrise
cocktail with a great tropical taste.
Watch the grenadine gently rise up the
glass to give a beautiful graded look.

1 PART ORANGE JUICE

1 PART PINEAPPLE JUICE

3 TBSP GRENADINE

WEDGE OF PINEAPPLE AND SLICE OF ORANGE

Pour orange juice and pineapple juice into a glass.
Trickle grenadine into juices until a delicate pink
layer forms on the bottom. Do not stir. Serve with a
pineapple wedge and orange slice. ▼

MISH MASH

Lovely refreshing mix of cranberries and
orange citrus flavors.

2 TBSP CRANBERRIES, WASHED

JUICE AND GRATED RIND OF 1 SATSUMA OR TANGERINE

150ML (⅔ CUP) WATER

1 TBSP SUGAR

TOP UP WITH SODA WATER

Place cranberries, grated rind and water into a pan.
Bring to the boil and simmer for five minutes. Stir in
sugar and satsuma juice, cool slightly and strain
through a sieve to squeeze out juice. Chill, pour into
a glass and top up with soda water. ▼

BILLY BUNTER

Marshmallow-pink with a citrussy froth
and a subtle banana side-kick.

1 RIPE BANANA, CHOPPED

1 PART ORANGE JUICE

1 PART WHIPPING CREAM

½ PART GRENADINE

Put banana and orange juice in a blender and whiz
until banana purées. Pour in cream and grenadine
and purée to a smooth warm pink color. Pour into a
glass and serve with a pink striped straw. ▼

✱ ORANGE NOG ✱

Opaque and orangey, a flavorful
cocktail with a macho touch of bitterness
in the background.

1 PART ORANGE JUICE

1 EGG, BEATEN

1 TSP SUGAR

DASH OF ANGOSTURA BITTERS

DROP OF VANILLA EXTRACT

Put all ingredients in a blender and whiz until
smooth. Chill and serve. ▼

To frost rim of a cocktail glass, dip into
lightly mixed egg white, then twist into
superfine sugar.

BLACKEYE

Gothic looking, dark currant flavored
drink.

1 PART COLA

1 TBSP BLACK CURRANT SYRUP

Pour cola into a glass and add syrup. Stir. ▮

Suit the glass to the cocktail: tall tumblers for
thirst quenching fizzes; short, chunky glasses
for thick, creamy, or rich tasting drinks;
cocktail glasses for exotic delicacies;
wineglasses for fruit mixtures.

DREAM MACHINE

Fresh peach whizzed in a blender with
sugar and cream to give a delicious
sherbet with dense frothy bubbles –
which stay!

FLESH OF 1 FRESH PEACH

1 TSP SUGAR

1 PART LIGHT CREAM

TOP UP WITH LEMONADE, CHILLED

WEDGE OF FRESH PEACH

Peel and halve peach. Place in a blender and whiz
up to a thin purée. Add sugar and taste for
sweetness. Pour into a glass, trickle in cream. Add
lemonade to the rim and watch the mixture froth up.
Decorate with a wedge of fresh peach and serve
chilled. ❗

ROLLER COASTER

Pale orange on top and deep rosy pink
underneath with a crushed pineapple
infusion.

½ PART CRUSHED PINEAPPLE

1 PART ORANGE JUICE

1 PART LEMONADE

1 TBSP GRENADINE

Spoon crushed pineapple into a glass. Pour over
orange juice and lemonade. Carefully pour in
grenadine to make a delicate pink layer at the
bottom of the glass, shading up to orange. ❧

KING SOLOMON'S MINE

Delicious, purple, fruity combination of
apricot, lime and black currant syrup.

FLESH OF ½ APRICOT

1 TSP SUPERFINE SUGAR

JUICE OF ½ LIME

1 PART BLACK CURRANT SYRUP

TOP UP WITH LEMONADE, CHILLED

FEW BLACK CURRANTS TO DECORATE

Cut apricot into small chunks, add sugar and lime
juice. Leave to soak for 30 minutes to infuse flavors.
Pour into a glass, splash in black currant syrup and
top up with lemonade. To decorate, float a few
black currants and a leaf if you can find one, on
top. ❧

ACE OF CLUBS

Frothy, bubbling black currant drink with
undertones of mint and lemon.

1 TBSP BLACK CURRANT SYRUP

1 TBSP MINT SYRUP

1 TBSP LEMON JUICE

TOP UP WITH SODA WATER

Pour black currant, mint and lemon juice into a
glass. Top up with soda water. 🍷

SUPER SOBER

Pale lemon-gold citrus drink, to cleanse
the palate.

JUICE OF 2 LIMES

1 TSP SUPERFINE SUGAR

JUICE OF ½ LEMON

1 EGG WHITE

CRUSHED ICE

CHERRY TO DECORATE

Dip rim of glass into lime juice, then into sugar for a
frosty rim. Shake remaining lime juice, lemon juice,
egg white with crushed ice. Strain into a glass and
decorate with a cherry. 🍸

Shaking a cocktail gives a cloudy drink,
stirring gives a clear drink.

STIR CRAZY

Mix apple and pears for a uniquely
quenching juice.

---

1 PART APPLE JUICE

---

1 PART PEAR JUICE

Mix two juices together. Stir and serve chilled. ⟋

MIDNIGHT COWBOY

Quirky mix of orange and cherry for a
pink and orange cocktail.

---

1 PART ORANGE JUICE

---

1 PART CHERRY JUICE

SLICE OF ORANGE AND CHERRY WITH STEM

Pour orange and cherry juice into a glass. Decorate
with orange slice and a cherry. ⟋

> Use cooled boiled water for ice cubes to
> make them crystal clear.

BLACK BELT

Mahogany drink with a plummy taste.

---

1 PART PRUNE JUICE

---

1 PART RED GRAPE JUICE

Mix prune and red grape juice. Serve. ◼

If regularly making fruity cocktails, invest in a fruit juicer it will save hours of squeezing by hand.

RUNNING SHORTS

Pretty salmon-pink drink packed with energy.

---

2 TBSP GRENADINE

---

1 PART ORANGE JUICE

---

1 EGG YOLK

---

1 ICE CUBE

Pour all ingredients into a shaker and shake for 30 seconds. Strain into a glass to serve. ☐

ANGELES MIST

Fruity, opaque and creamy pineapple cocktail with the palest orange tinge.

---

1 PART PINEAPPLE JUICE

---

1 PART LIGHT CREAM

JUICE OF ½ ORANGE

CRUSHED ICE

THIN SLICE OF PINEAPPLE TO DECORATE

Vigorously shake pineapple juice, cream and orange juice together in a cocktail shaker with some crushed ice. Strain into a glass and decorate with a pineapple slice. ☐

MIAMI VICE

Golden and creamy fizz.

FLESH OF 1 NECTARINE, DICED

1 PART LEMONADE

1 TSP BOTTLED SWEETENED LIME JUICE

1 TBSP WHIPPING CREAM

2 ICE CUBES

Whiz up all ingredients in a processor and serve. ▼

NEWTON'S NOGGIN

Pale green and slightly sparkling, crisp apple drink.

---

2 GREEN APPLES, CHOPPED

4 TBSP BOILING WATER

1 TSP LEMON JUICE

1 SUGAR CUBE

TOP UP WITH SPARKLING MINERAL WATER

APPLE SLICE TO DECORATE

Put apples in a heat-resistant pitcher and pour over water and lemon juice. Leave for five minutes. Pour into a blender and whiz up until it looks mushy. Strain juice through a sieve, using the back of a spoon. Cool, then chill. Pour into a glass. Add sugar cube and top up with mineral water. Float apple slice on top to serve. ■

SWEET AND SOUR

Orangey-yellow, fruity drink with a
piquant sweet and sour background.

---

1 PART APPLE JUICE

---

1 PART GRAPEFRUIT JUICE

JUICE OF ½ ORANGE

**2 ICE CUBES FROZEN WITH A WEDGE
OF GREEN APPLE IN EACH**

Pour apple, grapefruit and orange juice into a glass.
Add apple ice cubes and serve with a cocktail
stirrer. ▼

BELISHA BEACON

Brilliant-orange, sophisticated and
sensual drink.

FLESH OF 4 NECTARINES, DICED

JUICE OF 1 LARGE ORANGE

FEW ICE CUBES

Poach nectarines in orange juice until soft. Press
juice through a sieve. Chill. Pour over ice into a
glass. ▼

CHAPTER 7

LOOK-ALIKE DRINKS

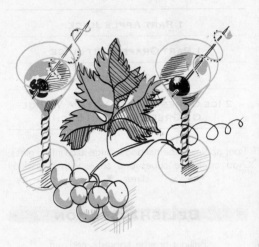

These drinks are non-alcoholic versions of classic cocktails. They taste just as good — and, on some occasions, some people may find it useful that they look just the same.

IRISH COFFEE

1 TSP INSTANT COFFEE

150ML (⅔ CUP) BOILING WATER

1 TBSP HONEY

2 TBSP WHIPPING CREAM

Mix coffee, water and honey and stir until dissolved. Pour into a heat-resistant glass and carefully pour in cream over the back of a spoon to form a creamy layer on top.

BRANDY ALEXANDER

1 TSP INSTANT COFFEE

1 TBSP BOILING WATER

1 TSP LIGHT BROWN SUGAR

1 PART WHIPPING CREAM

2 ICE CUBES

PINCH OF GROUND NUTMEG

Dissolve coffee in water with sugar. Cool. Shake with cream and ice and strain into a champagne flute. Sprinkle with nutmeg.

* SINGAPORE SLING *

1 TBSP LEMON JUICE

1 PART NON-ALCOHOLIC WHITE WINE

1 TBSP GRENADINE

2 ICE CUBES FROZEN WITH FRESH CHERRIES

Pour lemon juice and wine into a glass. Stir in grenadine and serve with cherry ice cubes.

* KIR *

2 TBSP BLACK CURRANT SYRUP

1 PART NON-ALCOHOLIC SPARKLING WHITE WINE

Pour syrup into a glass and stir in wine to serve.

BLACK RUSSIAN

1 TSP INSTANT COFFEE

1 TBSP BOILING WATER

JUICE OF ½ LIME

TOP UP WITH COLA

Dissolve coffee in water. Cool. Add lime juice and pour into a glass. Top up with cola. ❦

✳ BUCKS FIZZ ✳

Refreshing and sophisticated bubbly.

1 PART NON-ALCOHOLIC SPARKLING WHITE WINE

1 PART ORANGE JUICE, CHILLED

Pour wine into champagne flute and top up with orange juice. ❦

PINA COLADA

1 TBSP LIGHT BROWN SUGAR

1 PART COCONUT MILK

1 PART CRUSHED PINEAPPLE

CRUSHED ICE

WEDGE OF PINEAPPLE TO DECORATE

Put all ingredients into a blender and whiz for 30 seconds. Pour into a glass and serve with a straw and a wedge of pineapple. ❦

★ COPS AND ROBBERS ★

Dazzling, clear, bronze with a manly hint
of bitters.

DASH OF ANGOSTURA BITTERS

1 PART NON-ALCOHOLIC SPARKLING
WHITE WINE

Pour a dash of bitters into a glass and top up with
wine. ♈

> For free-flow ice cubes, turn frozen cubes
> out onto a baking sheet and separate.
> Re-freeze for 15 minutes then tip into a
> polythene bag. Repeat with remaining
> ice cubes.

★ SUPER SPRITZER ★

Such a delicious refreshing spritzer,
you'll prefer this to the real thing.

2 ICE CUBES, FROZEN WITH COCKTAIL
CHERRIES

FEW DROPS OF ANGOSTURA BITTERS

1 PART NON-ALCOHOLIC WHITE WINE,
CHILLED

1 PART SODA WATER

First make the ice cubes. Place a cocktail cherry in
each section of ice cube tray. Top up with water.
Freeze. Put Angostura bitters in a glass and swirl
around to coat the inside. Add wine and top up with
soda. Serve with cherry ice cubes. ♈

PERNOD AND BLACK

Aniseed flavored black currant drink.

---

1 TBSP DRIED ANISEED

---

1 TBSP BOILING WATER

---

2 TBSP BLACK CURRANT SYRUP

---

1 TSP WHIPPING CREAM

ICE CUBES

Infuse aniseed in water for five minutes. Strain into a glass. Cool. Add syrup, cream and ice. Stir. 🍸

✦ KNIGHTSBRIDGE ✦

Sophisticated and elegant lime fizz with a subtle hint of bitterness. The non-alcoholic tipple of British aristocrats.

---

1 PART CREAM SODA

JUICE OF ½ LIME

DASH OF ANGOSTURA BITTERS

CRUSHED ICE

SLICE OF LIME

Mix cream soda, lime juice and bitters in a pitcher. Pour over ice into a glass. Decorate with a thin slice of lime. 🍸

CHAPTER 8

SODA &
FIZZY DRINKS

The best refreshers in the world. These are
sparkling and fizzy quenchers for the whole
family. Long drinks with the delicate flavors
of fruits and spices, sometimes enriched with
ice cream provide an everyday range of
drinks with a difference.

✦ GLACIER ✦

Fluorescent, radiant green, refreshing
palate cleansing drink.

---

1 PART NON-ALCOHOLIC SPARKLING
WHITE WINE

---

1 TBSP MINT SYRUP

DASH OF LEMON JUICE

Pour wine into a glass, add syrup and lemon juice
and stir. ♟

GUNPOWDER PLOT

Fizzy, sparkling, sherbety explosion.

1 PART LEMONADE, CHILLED

DASH OF FRESHLY SQUEEZED LEMON JUICE

1 SCOOP LEMON SORBET (SHERBET)

SLICE OF LEMON AND CHERRY WITH A STEM

Pour lemonade into a glass and add lemon juice. Add a scoop of sorbet and decorate with a twisted lemon slice and cherry. ▼

WHITE LIAR

Clear, sparkling drink flecked with orange shreds. Refreshing and frisky with a peppery bite. This unusual and stimulating taste comes from the syrup in a jar of stem ginger. Use the ginger as a garnish.

2 TBSP STEM GINGER SYRUP

JUICE OF ½ ORANGE

TOP UP WITH SPARKLING MINERAL WATER

ORANGE SLICE AND A NUGGET OF STEM GINGER

Spoon out the syrupy juice from a jar of stem ginger, mix with orange juice and top up with mineral water. Pour into a chilled glass. Decorate with a twist of orange and ginger on a cocktail stick. ▼

Keep a good supply of lemons, oranges, ice cubes, eggs, lemonade and soda for instant drinks.

MICKEY MOUSE SODA

Ice cream drink with a zigzag of strawberry syrup across vanilla ice cream and a brown frothy topping.

1 PART COLA

1 SCOOP VANILLA ICE CREAM

DRIZZLE OF STRAWBERRY SYRUP

Pour cola into a glass. Carefully place a scoop of ice cream on top. Drizzle over syrup in a zigzag pattern to decorate. ▮

HENRY'S ORCHARD

Henry VIII had one of the first apple orchards in England. This was his favorite apple drink. Clear and sparkling, two-toned – pink on the bottom and pale orange on top. Serve chilled.

1 PART APPLE JUICE

½ PART LEMON JUICE

1 PART GINGER ALE

½ PART GRENADINE

Pour apple and lemon juice into a glass. Top up with ginger ale and carefully drizzle in grenadine for a delicate rosy pink layered, but clear drink. ▼

✶ STORMY WEATHER ✶

Cloudy and mysterious with a light
almond flavor.

1 TBSP ALMOND SYRUP

1 PART NON-ALCOHOLIC SPARKLING
WHITE WINE

Pour almond syrup into a glass. Top up with wine.
Stir. 🍷

DOMINO

Richly fruity. Drink it as it is – or dilute
with soda water to taste.

1 PART PRUNE JUICE

1 PART PINEAPPLE JUICE

TOP UP WITH SODA WATER

Pour prune and pineapple juice into a glass. Top up
with soda water. 🍷

OLYMPIC GOLD

Clear, sunrise-pink layer at the bottom
rising to gold.

1 PART PASSION FRUIT JUICE

1 PART SPARKLING MINERAL WATER

1 TBSP STRAWBERRY SYRUP

Pour passion fruit juice and water into a glass and
drizzle strawberry syrup on top. 🍷

SILVER SHADOW

Delicate, faintly opaque silvery color
with an infusion of finely chopped mint.

---

1 PART GRAPEFRUIT JUICE

DASH OF BOTTLED SWEETENED LIME JUICE

1 TBSP SUGAR

1 TBSP FRESH MINT, FINELY CHOPPED

TOP UP WITH SODA WATER

FEW FRESH MINT LEAVES

Place grapefruit, lime and sugar in a pan and bring
to the boil. Add the mint and allow to cool for a
delicate minty taste. Strain and pour into a glass, top
up with soda and decorate with mint leaves. ▪

PIRATE'S SAVIOUR

Refreshing lime quencher with a delicate
pale straw color.

JUICE OF 1 LIME

2 TSP SUPERFINE SUGAR

TOP UP WITH SODA WATER

1 SUGAR CUBE

FRESHLY SQUEEZED ORANGE JUICE

Squeeze out as much juice from the lime as possible.
Pour into a glass, stir in sugar and top up with soda
water. Soak sugar cube with orange juice and add
just before serving. ▼

POT BELLY

Opaque white, thirst quencher with a
frothy head and the subtle oriental taste
of ginger.

1 PART GINGER BEER

1 TBSP FRESHLY SQUEEZED
LEMON JUICE

1 PART LEMONADE

Mix ginger beer and lemon juice and pour into a
glass. Top up with lemonade. ▼

> Stir gently with a cocktail stirrer or bar
> spoon after adding anything fizzy, or the
> bubbles will disappear.

EIFFEL TOWER

Tall, refreshing long drink. Palest
pastel green and clear with
a delicate citrusy flavor.

1 LARGE GREEN APPLE

150ML (⅔ CUP) BOILING WATER

½ TSP SUGAR

TOP UP WITH LEMONADE

ICE CUBES

Chop apple and place in a bowl. Pour over boiling
water and add sugar. Stand for ten minutes and
strain into a pitcher. Cool. Serve in glasses topped
up with lemonade and ice cubes. ▼

LEAP FROG

Vivid green, sparkling and peppery.

---

1 PART PASSION FRUIT JUICE

---

1 PART GINGER ALE

---

1 TBSP MINT SYRUP

Mix passion fruit juice and ginger ale in a glass. Stir in mint syrup. ▼

✱ SHERINGHAM ✱

Clear, lemony and refreshing sparkling drink.

---

1 PART NON-ALCOHOLIC SPARKLING WHITE WINE

---

1 PART LEMONADE

---

2 SLICES OF CUCUMBER AND SPRIG OF FRESH MINT TO DECORATE

Pour wine and lemonade into a glass. Decorate with cucumber and mint leaves. ▼

TOM AND CHERRY

Sherbety and brilliant pink, with a sparkling fizzy taste.

---

1 PART CHERRY SODA

---

2 SCOOPS VANILLA ICE CREAM

Whiz up in a blender until frothy. Pour into a glass and serve with a pink cocktail umbrella. ▼

POCA POLA

If you make only one drink from this book it has to be this – then ask your friends to guess what it is. A small clue. It's deep brown, slightly peppery, fizzy and frothy. Any resemblance to cola is totally intentional.

1 PART PRUNE JUICE

1 PART GINGER ALE

1 TBSP COLD INDIAN TEA

Pour all ingredients into a glass and stir. ▾

BLUSHER

Pretty, pink and transparent strawberry fizz.

1 PART STRAWBERRY SYRUP

JUICE OF ½ LEMON

TOP UP WITH SPARKLING MINERAL WATER

WHOLE STRAWBERRY TO DECORATE

Pour syrup into a glass. Add freshly squeezed lemon juice and stir. Top up with mineral water and decorate with a whole strawberry. ■

Freeze leftover blueberries, raspberries and loganberries on open trays then store in sealed polythene bags. Use for decoration or ice cubes. See garnishes section in the introduction.

BLACK CURRANT SODA

Delicate shade of lavender and daintly
brushed with the taste of black currant.

---

2 TBSP BLACK CURRANT SYRUP

TOP UP WITH SODA WATER

ICE CUBES

Pour syrup in a glass. Top up with soda and add ice.
Stir. ❦

ECLIPSE

Fizzy and inky dark refresher.

---

1 PART COLA

---

1 PART GINGER BEER

CRUSHED ICE

Mix together in a glass and serve over crushed
ice. ❦

DICK TURPIN

Pale orange drink with a bitter orange
tang and a heady perfume.

---

1 PART APRICOT JUICE

---

1 PART BITTER LEMON

SLICE OF APRICOT TO DECORATE

Mix apricot juice and bitter lemon and pour into a
glass. Decorate with an apricot slice. ❦

WIMBLEDON

Fragrant fruit and vegetable cup with
pepperiness and fizz. Refreshing on a
hot, sporty day.

---

1 PART ORANGE JUICE

1 PART GINGER BEER

SLICE OF CUCUMBER, RED APPLE AND ORANGE CUT THINLY WITH THE SKIN LEFT ON

ICE CUBES

Pour orange juice into a glass. Add ice and top with
ginger beer. Drop in cucumber, apple and orange
to decorate. ▼

PEP UP

Brilliant orange, palate-cleansing and
refreshing *frizzante* drink with a peppery
background.

---

2 TBSP STEM GINGER SYRUP

1 TSP SUGAR

SQUIRT OF LEMON JUICE

1 PART ORANGE JUICE

1 PART TONIC WATER

Dip rim of glass in a saucer filled with stem ginger
syrup, then twist into sugar to make a sparkling
sugar edge. Spoon syrup from jar of stem ginger
into a glass. Mix with lemon and orange juice.
Carefully top up with tonic water not disturbing the
sugar rim. ▼

SWEET NOTHING

Gently spiced with a hint of lemon.

1 TBSP MAPLE SYRUP

1 TBSP LEMON JUICE

1 PART GINGER ALE

STEM GINGER TO DECORATE

Mix syrup and lemon juice in a glass. Top up with ginger ale and serve with a cocktail stick threaded with a thin slice of stem ginger. ▰

AZTEC GOLD

Sweet, slightly fizzy and transparent pale gold quencher with a touch of spice.

1 PART APPLE JUICE

3 WHOLE CLOVES

PINCH OF GROUND CINNAMON

1 TSP HONEY

1 PART TONIC WATER

Heat apple juice gently with cloves, cinnamon and honey for five minutes. Leave to cool completely in the pan, then chill. Pour into a glass and top up with tonic water. ♟

To frost rim of a cocktail glass, dip into lightly mixed egg white, then twist into superfine sugar.

WEEPING WILLOW

Palest green and dainty drink.

2 TBSP BOTTLED SWEETENED LIME JUICE

1 PART SPARKLING MINERAL WATER

2 SCOOPS VANILLA ICE CREAM

Whiz up all ingredients in a blender for 30 seconds until frothy. Pour into a chilled glass. ♈

ROSY CHEEKS

Vivid, rosy red, and refreshing.

1 PART RED GRAPE JUICE

1 PART SPARKLING APPLE JUICE

Pour grape juice into a glass and top up with apple juice. ♈

RUBY

Clear red, fruity and peppery.

1 PART RED GRAPE JUICE

1 PART GINGER ALE

HALVED SEEDLESS BLACK GRAPE TO DECORATE

ICE CUBES

Pour both ingredients into a glass and serve with grape and ice. ♈

Add lemonade, soda or sparkling mineral water just before serving to avoid a flat drink.

SUNSET STRIP

Fizzy, gold-orange drink with a whisper of ginger in the background.

1 PART ORANGE JUICE

1 PART GINGER ALE

1 PART SPARKLING MINERAL WATER

CHERRY AND A SLICE OF ORANGE TO DECORATE

ICE CUBES

Pour orange juice into a glass and top up with ginger ale and mineral water. Decorate with a cherry and orange slice skewered to a cocktail stick. Add an ice cube to serve. ❧

SHOCKING

Radiant-pink, slightly sparkling with a delicious summery flavor.

1 PART CREAM SODA

1 PART RED GRAPE JUICE

DASH OF LEMON JUICE

WEDGE OF LEMON TO DECORATE

Mix everything together in a glass. Serve with a wedge of lemon. ❧

FIRE EATER

Peppery apple drink with translucent color.

1 PART GINGER BEER

2 PARTS SPARKLING APPLE JUICE

ICE CUBES

Pour ginger beer and apple juice into a glass and serve with ice. ❦

BLACKBURN

Marshmallow taste and dark and frothy in appearance.

1 PART COLA

DASH OF VANILLA EXTRACT

ICE CUBES

Fill a glass with cola and stir in vanilla extract. Serve with a straw and ice. ◼

RED ALERT

Black currant pink fizz, frisky and sweet.

1 PART CHERRY SODA

1 PART RED GRAPE JUICE

CHERRY AND RED GRAPE TO DECORATE

Mix both together in a glass. Serve with a cherry and a grape on a cocktail stick. ❦

✱ BAGDAD ✱

Pale amber with the subtle flavor of
passion fruit.

1 PART NON-ALCOHOLIC SPARKLING WHITE WINE

1 PART PASSION FRUIT JUICE

Pour both into a glass and stir. 🍷

PINK PANTHER

Brilliant pink and slightly sparkling with
the taste of cherries.

1 PART CHERRY SODA

1 PART PINEAPPLE JUICE

WEDGE OF PINEAPPLE AND CHERRY TO DECORATE

Mix together and pour into a glass. Decorate with
pineapple wedge and cherry. 🍸

✱ FLAMINGO FLAME ✱

Fluorescent pink, tangy and sparkling.

1 PART NON-ALCOHOLIC SPARKLING WHITE WINE

1 PART GRAPEFRUIT JUICE

DASH OF GRENADINE

Pour wine and grapefruit juice into a glass. Add
grenadine and watch it turn pink. 🍸

ICE CREAM SODA

300ML (1 ¼ CUPS) SODA WATER

1 SCOOP VANILLA ICE CREAM

Whiz up soda and ice cream in a blender until frothy. Pour into a glass to serve. ▼

SNOW WHITE

Fruity fizz, a delicate shade of pink.

FLESH OF 1 PLUM, CHOPPED

1 PART GUAVA JUICE

1 PART LEMONADE

SLICE OF PLUM TO DECORATE

ICE CUBES

Whiz up plum and guava juice in a blender. Strain into a glass and top up with lemonade. Decorate with plum slice and serve with ice. ▼

LEXINGTON

Sparkling indulgence.

1 PART PRUNE JUICE

1 PART CREAM SODA

1 SCOOP VANILLA ICE CREAM

Mix prune juice and cream soda in a glass. Add a scoop of ice cream and serve immediately. ▼

CHAPTER 9

VEGETABLE JUICES

Healthy vegetable juices are internationally popular. These include deliciously rich cocktails such as Aztec King made from avocado, plus a stimulating hot and herby tomato drink, as well as carrot and cucumber juices. Madonna is a superb alcohol-free Bloody Mary. Try it and see who needs alcohol.

COOLING CUCUMBER

Bright green, use as a drink on its own, or to add to other vegetable drinks.

½ CUCUMBER

150ML (⅔ CUP) WATER, CHILLED

PINCH OF SALT

Peel and chop cucumber and place in a blender with water and salt. Blend until smooth. Pour into a chilled glass. ∎

PALE FACE

Thick, smooth and sensuously creamy. A
sublime and unexpectedly delicious mix
of carrot juice and orange with a touch
of paprika spice.

---

1 PART CARROT JUICE

---

1 PART ORANGE JUICE

---

1 PART HEAVY CREAM

PINCH OF PAPRIKA

Put carrot, orange juice and cream in a blender and
whiz for 30 seconds. Pour into glass and sprinkle
over paprika. 🍷

FRAZZLE

Pale green, creamy and seductively rich.

½ AVOCADO, CHOPPED

---

1 TSP LEMON JUICE

---

2 TBSP STRAWBERRY SYRUP

150ML (⅔ CUP) APPLE JUICE

150ML (⅔ CUP) SPARKLING MINERAL WATER

Whiz up all ingredients, except water in a blender
until smooth. Pour into a glass and top up with
mineral water. 🍸

> Always add lemon juice to avocado drinks
> to avoid discoloration.

PILLAR-BOX

Scarlet, salty, savoury drink. A perfect
aperitif. Use the brine from a jar of black
olives as seasoning and use a stick of
celery as a stirrer. Eat it afterwards.

---

2 PARTS TOMATO JUICE

---

1 PART BLACK OLIVE JUICE

---

1 THIN STICK OF CELERY

BLACK OLIVE

Pour tomato juice into a glass, add olive brine. Give
it a good stir with the celery, then decorate with a
black olive, leaving celery in the glass. ▪

HEATWAVE

Thick and stimulating tomato drink with
heat and herbiness.

---

2 TOMATOES, SKINNED, SEEDED AND CHOPPED

150ML (⅔ CUP) PLAIN YOGURT

DASH OF TABASCO

½ TSP SUGAR

FRESHLY GROUND BLACK PEPPER

WEDGE OF LEMON DIPPED INTO FINELY CHOPPED FRESH BASIL

Blend all ingredients except garnish in a blender.
Chill. Pour into a glass and secure lemon wedge to
rim with a cocktail stick. Serve with a good squeeze
of lemon juice stirred in. ▪

MADONNA

Ripe and savoury, a rich-tasting spicy
drink with no shame.

1 PART TOMATO JUICE

DASH OF WORCESTERSHIRE SAUCE

DASH OF TABASCO

DASH OF LEMON JUICE

PINCH OF SALT

PINCH OF PAPRIKA

2 ICE CUBES

**CELERY STICK WITH LEAVES, WASHED
AND DRIED**

Mix everything together except celery. Pour into a
glass, add ice and serve with a celery stick for
stirring. ▼

CARROT JUICE

Packed with vitamin A, this healthy drink
is refreshing and delicious, too.

4 LARGE CARROTS, PEELED AND GRATED

JUICE OF ½ LEMON

300ML (1¼ CUPS) WATER

DASH OF TABASCO

Purée everything in a blender until smooth. Strain to
squeeze out all the juice. Add Tabasco and chill
before serving. ◼

BUNNY HOP

Delicate carrot drink with a thick texture
and packed with vitamins. A tasty
savoury treat with a discreet touch of
heat in the background.

---

1 PART CARROT JUICE

---

1 PART ORANGE JUICE

LARGE DASH OF TABASCO

CARROT CURL TO DECORATE

Mix carrot and orange juice and stir in Tabasco.
Pour into a glass, peel and wash a carrot and
carefully pare a thin strip. Plunge into cold water
and leave until curled. Spear with a cocktail stick
and use as decoration. ■

BLOCKBUSTER

Savoury, nourishing and healthy
vegetable drink of tomato and carrot
juice, spiked with Worcestershire sauce
and decorated with a cocktail onion on
a stick. Almost a meal in a glass.

---

1 PART TOMATO JUICE

---

1 PART CARROT JUICE

DASH OF WORCESTERSHIRE SAUCE

SPRINKLE OF CAYENNE PEPPER

COCKTAIL ONION

Pour tomato and carrot juice into a glass and stir.
Add a dash of Worcestershire sauce. Spear an
onion with a cocktail stick and lay across glass. ■

AZTEC KING

Ancient Aztecs first cultivated avocados
and may well have made this nutritious,
pale green drink.

½ AVOCADO, CHOPPED

1 TBSP HONEY

JUICE OF ½ LEMON

150ML (⅔ CUP) SODA WATER

Whiz up everything in a blender until smooth. Pour
into a glass and top up with soda. ▆

HEALTHY COOLER

Jungle-green vegetable drink.
Refreshing and tangy with a hint of
sharpness.

2IN (5CM) PIECE OF CUCUMBER, PEELED

DASH OF FRESHLY SQUEEZED LEMON JUICE

2 PARTS WHITE GRAPE JUICE

CRUSHED ICE

SLICE OF CUCUMBER

Put cucumber into a blender and whiz up to a pulp.
Strain. Pour cucumber juice into a glass, add a dash
of lemon juice and top up with grape juice. Serve
over crushed ice and decorate with a slice of
cucumber. ❢

CHAPTER 10

HERBAL DRINKS

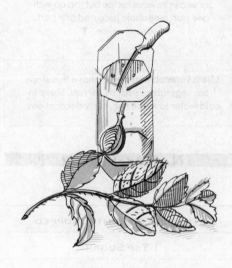

Mostly made by infusing the herb to extract
the most flavor. Water, sometimes boiling, is
poured over and the mix left to stand to
flavor and color the water. These drinks
have a refreshing country taste.

PYTHAGORUS

Aromatic, sparkling fresh and delicate
gooseberry-green.

2 TBSP FRESH CORIANDER, CHOPPED

150ML (⅔ CUP) BOILING WATER

150ML (⅔ CUP) BITTER LEMON

Infuse coriander in boiling water for 15 minutes.
Whiz up in a blender, then strain into a glass. Top up
with bitter lemon. ▼

ISOSCELES

Same as previous recipe but top up with
one part pineapple juice and one part
orange juice. ▼

Use a vegetable peeler to shave thin strips
from vegetables such as carrots. Steep in
cold water to make thin, curly decorations.

NAMBY-PAMBY

Clear green, sparkling mint infusion.

---

4 TBSP FRESH MINT, CHOPPED

1 TSP SUGAR

150ML (⅔ CUP) BOILING WATER

JUICE OF ½ LEMON

TOP UP WITH GINGER ALE

1 EGG WHITE, LIGHTLY WHISKED

1 TBSP SUPERFINE SUGAR

CRUSHED ICE

MINT LEAVES AND 4 CHERRIES TO DECORATE

Put mint and sugar in a heat-resistant pitcher and
pour over boiling water. Leave to cool. Add lemon
juice and strain into a clean pitcher. Top up with
ginger ale. Dip rim of glass into egg white, and then
into sugar. Put crushed ice into a glass and pour
drink over. Decorate with mint leaves and
cherries. ▼

JAILHOUSE ROCK

Rust-colored, sparkling apple and mint
taste. Serve chilled over ice cubes.

---

3 SPRIGS OF FRESH MINT

150ML (⅔ CUP) BOILING WATER

ICE CUBES

---

1 PART APPLE JUICE, CHILLED

---

1 PART SODA WATER

FRESH MINT LEAVES AND APPLE SLICE TO DECORATE

Infuse mint in water for 15 minutes. Whiz up in a blender until water goes green. Strain, using the back of a spoon to press out liquid. Cool, then chill. Pour into a glass over ice cubes, and top with apple juice and soda water. Decorate with fresh mint and a slice of green apple. ■

★ BITTER MINT ★

Mint infusion with a dash of bitters.

---

3 SPRIGS OF FRESH MINT

150ML (⅔ CUP) BOILING WATER

FEW DROPS OF ANGOSTURA BITTERS

TOP UP WITH BITTER LEMON

Infuse mint in water for 15 minutes. Whiz up in a blender until water goes green. Strain, using the back of a spoon to press out liquid. Cool, then chill. Pour into a glass, add Angostura bitters and top up with bitter lemon. ■

BOLD BORIS

Ancient Greeks said that borage
made you cheerful. Try this golden drink
and see.

2 PARTS APPLE JUICE

½ LEMON, SLICED

1 TBSP FRESH BORAGE LEAVES, CHOPPED

1 PART ORANGE JUICE

2 PARTS SODA WATER

BORAGE LEAVES TO DECORATE

Place apple juice, lemon and chopped borage in a
bowl. Leave to infuse for at least one hour. Strain
into a pitcher, squeezing the juice out from the
lemons. Mix with orange juice and chill. Pour into a
glass, add soda and top with borage leaves. ▼

MINT CONDITION

Pale straw-colored drink with a fresh
mint taste and a background of ginger
spice.

3 SPRIGS OF FRESH MINT

150ML (⅔ CUP) BOILING WATER

TOP UP WITH GINGER ALE

Infuse mint in water for 15 minutes. Whiz up in a
blender until it colors the water and is finely
chopped. Strain, using the back of a spoon to press
out liquid. Cool, then chill. Pour into a glass and top
up with ginger ale. ■

MR COOL

Topaz-colored, slightly fizzy and
aromatically citrussy.

---

3 TBSP FRESH PARSLEY, CHOPPED

3 TBSP BOILING WATER

1 PART ORANGE JUICE

1 PART BITTER LEMON

FEW ICE CUBES

SPRIG OF PARSLEY TO DECORATE

Mix chopped parsley with water and leave to infuse
until cold. Strain juice into a pitcher. Add orange
juice and bitter lemon. Pour into a glass, add ice and
decorate with parsley. ❧

✶ SPIROS ✶

Marjoram was known as 'joy of the
mountains' by the Ancient Greeks.
Bitter, aromatic and sparkling.

---

1 TBSP FRESH MARJORAM, CHOPPED

1 PART GRAPEFRUIT JUICE

1 PART SPARKLING MINERAL WATER

DASH OF ANGOSTURA BITTERS

SPRIG OF MARJORAM TO DECORATE

Chill chopped marjoram and grapefruit juice
together for at least one hour. Strain and pour into a
glass. Top with mineral water and bitters, stir and
decorate with marjoram. ❧

Sprinkle a pinch of paprika or cayenne pepper over savory drinks for a hint of spicy heat.

COLD CURER

Crocodile-green with sweet herbiness. Citrussy, fizzy and herby – you can feel it doing you good.

---

3 SPRIGS OF PARSLEY, WASHED AND STALKS TRIMMED

150ML (⅔ CUP) BOILING WATER

JUICE OF 1 LEMON

---

1 TBSP HONEY

TOP UP WITH SPARKLING MINERAL WATER

SLICE OF LEMON TO DECORATE

Infuse parsley in water for 15 minutes. Pour into a blender and whiz up until parsley breaks up. Add lemon juice and stir in honey. Cool and chill. Pour into a glass, top up with mineral water and serve with a slice of lemon. Or top up with ginger ale, or white grape juice and soda instead of mineral water. ❦

CHAPTER 11

TEA & COFFEE

Really exciting drinks in this section made from teas and coffees. Ranging from long, refreshing thirst quenchers to variations on iced coffee, some with fruity additions. Plus some sophisticated tea drinks, long and short.

CASABLANCA

Iced coffee with a caramel taste.

---

1 TSP INSTANT COFFEE

---

4 TBSP BOILING WATER

---

1 TBSP MAPLE SYRUP

150ML (⅔ CUP) MILK, CHILLED

Dissolve coffee in water. Stir in maple syrup and chill. Pour into a glass and top up with milk. Stir. ♟

OLDE ENGLISH TEA

Elegant and clear khaki drink. Serve
chilled with mint ice cubes.

FRESH MINT LEAVES FOR MINT
ICE CUBES

300ML (1 ¼ CUPS) BOILING WATER

2 TBSP FRESH MINT, CHOPPED

1 TBSP HONEY, OR TO TASTE

First make the ice cubes. Place a washed mint leaf in
each section of an ice cube tray. Top up with water.
Freeze. Pour water over mint and allow to stand for
ten minutes. Stir in honey until melted. Chill and
strain into a glass. Add mint leaf ice cubes. ▼

ALI BABA

Smooth and sensuous, creamy coffee
drink.

1 TSP INSTANT COFFEE

1 TBSP BOILING WATER

1 SCOOP COFFEE ICE CREAM

300ML (1 ¼ CUPS) PINEAPPLE JUICE

Dissolve coffee in boiling water. Blend with ice
cream in a blender until smooth. Pour into a glass
and top up with pineapple juice. ■

For the best results, stir clear drinks and
shake cream, fruit juice and egg white
mixtures.

ICED COFFEE

An International favorite

1 TBSP SUGAR

150ML (⅔ CUP) STRONG COLD COFFEE

1 TSP LEMON JUICE

CRUSHED ICE

150ML (⅔ CUP) SODA WATER

SLICE OF LEMON

Mix sugar, coffee and lemon juice until sugar dissolves. Pour into a glass, add ice and soda and serve with a lemon slice. 🍸

Use cooled boiled water for ice cubes to make them crystal clear.

BRONZE AGE

Light, refreshing and creamy coffee.

2 TSP INSTANT COFFEE

150ML (⅔ CUP) BOILING WATER

SUGAR TO TASTE

2 ICE CUBES

2 TBSP WHIPPING CREAM

Mix coffee and water. Stir in sugar to taste while mix is still hot. Cool, pour over ice cubes into a glass. Pour in cream. 🍸

ARCTIC FREEZE

Refreshing iced mint tea.

---

1 MINT TEA BAG

150ML (2/3 CUP) BOILING WATER

CRUSHED ICE

SPRIG OF FRESH MINT

SLICE OF LEMON

Infuse mint tea in boiling water for three minutes. Cool and strain over crushed ice into a glass. Decorate with mint sprig and a lemon slice. ♆

GREAT WALL

Dainty refresher based on jasmine tea and ginger.

---

1 TSP JASMINE TEA LEAVES

150ML (2/3 CUP) BOILING WATER

150ML (2/3 CUP) GINGER ALE

TWIST OF LEMON

ICE CUBE

Infuse tea leaves in water for one minute. Strain into a pitcher and cool. Pour into a glass with ginger ale and decorate with a slice of lemon. ♆

> The term infusion means steeping the herb or tea leaves in hot or boiling water to extract the flavour.

TAJ MAHAL

Spicy Indian tea punch.
Makes 600ml (2½ cups)

600ML (2½ CUPS) WATER

---

2 CARDAMOMS

---

2 WHOLE CLOVES

---

1 CINNAMON STICK

---

2 TEA BAGS (INDIAN TEA)

---

3 TBSP MILK

Pour water into a pan. Add spices. Cover, bring to the boil then add tea and simmer for five minutes. Add milk, bring back to the boil then strain into heat-resistant glasses. 🥄

BEVERLEY HILLS

Pale, golden and frothy drink based on mint tea. Sweet and minty with a medicinal scent of honey.

150ML (⅔ CUP) BOILING WATER

---

1 MINT TEA BAG

---

1 TBSP LEMON JUICE

---

1 TBSP HONEY

SODA WATER TO TASTE

Pour boiling water over mint tea bag and leave to infuse for three minutes. Remove and stir in lemon juice and honey. Chill. Pour into a glass and add soda to taste. 🍸

Serve cocktails with small savouries, biscuits and canapes – never with a full meal.

Brown Sugar

Sensuous and sophisticated, a velvety smooth and creamy coffee drink.

1 Tsp Instant Coffee

2 Tbsp Hot Water

2 Parts Light Cream

1 Tbsp Honey

Crushed Ice

Melt coffee granules in water and mix to a smooth paste. Leave until cold. Stir in cream and honey and pour over crushed ice into a glass.

Tahiti Trance

Exotic coffee cocktail flavored with pineapple.

1 Part Freshly Brewed Coffee, Chilled

1 Part Pineapple Juice

1 Scoop Coffee Ice Cream

Wedge Of Fresh Pineapple To Decorate

Whiz up all ingredients in a blender for 30 seconds. Pour into a glass and decorate with a wedge of fresh pineapple.

SUMMERHOUSE CUP

Delicious, fragrant iced tea for sultry
summer days and balmy nights. Use any
tea you fancy for variations in flavor
and color.
Makes 2 liters

---

2 LITERS (9 CUPS) WATER

---

3 TBSP LOOSE TEA

---

2 LARGE SPRIGS OF FRESH MINT

150G (¾ CUP) SUGAR

---

1 ORANGE

---

1 LEMON

Bring 1 liter of water to the boil and add tea and one
sprig of mint. Simmer for five minutes. Strain and set
aside to cool. In a large glass pitcher, mix sugar and
other sprig of mint (broken up with stem) and mash
very well with a wooden spoon. Cut the orange and
lemon into quarters, squeeze the juice into pitcher,
then add the orange and lemon sections to pitcher
and mash well with wooden spoon. Add cooled tea
and remaining liter of cold water. Chill and
serve. ▼

CHAPTER 12

CHOCOLATE & MALT DRINKS

Sensuous and velvety drinks based on chocolate and malted milk. All irresistible, but not recommended for those on a calorie controlled diet.

MINTE CARLO

Speckled and creamy mint drink topped with green bubbles.

---

1 PART MINT CHOCOLATE ICE CREAM

---

1 PART BUTTERMILK

---

1 PART LEMONADE

Whiz up ice cream and buttermilk in a blender until smooth. Pour into a glass and top up with lemonade. ▼

RIP VAN WINKLE

Creamy, chocolate mint milk drink.
Perfect for after dinner. Soothing and
soporific with a scrumptious real
chocolaty taste.

6 SQUARES UNSWEETENED CHOCOLATE

300ML (1 ¼ CUPS) MILK

1 TBSP LIGHT CREAM

2 TBSP MINT SYRUP

Put chocolate and milk into a pan and gently heat
until chocolate melts. Whisk to froth up. Cool. Stir in
cream and mint syrup. Serve. ▪

POLTERGEIST

Ghostly-white, creamy vanilla drink with
a sweet malty taste.

150ML (⅔ CUP) MILK, CHILLED

2 LARGE SCOOPS VANILLA ICE CREAM

2 DROPS VANILLA EXTRACT

1 TBSP MALTED MILK POWDER

Pour milk into a blender. Add ice cream, vanilla and
malt and blend until smooth and frothy. ▪

Don't own a processor? – blend cocktail in a
bowl with a hand mixer. Crush ice by
wrapping in a clean tea towel and hitting
with a rolling pin.

CHOCABLOK

Scrumptious, hot chocolate.

---

2 TBSP COCOA POWDER

---

2 TBSP BOILING WATER

---

1 TBSP HONEY

---

5 TBSP WHIPPING CREAM

---

1 TBSP GRATED CHOCOLATE

Put cocoa, water, honey and 3 tbsp cream in a pan. Heat until honey has melted. Pour into heat-resistant glass. Top with remaining cream and grated chocolate.

STRAWBERRY FAIR

Milky-pink and scrumptious with a malty taste.

300ML (1¼ CUPS) MILK, CHILLED

---

1 TBSP MALTED MILK POWDER

---

2 LARGE SCOOPS STRAWBERRY ICE CREAM

STRAWBERRY SYRUP TO DECORATE

Blend milk with malt and ice cream in a blender until smooth. Pour into a glass and drizzle strawberry syrup on the top before serving.

> Be sure to use toasted nuts for sprinkling over drinks for a better flavor and appearance.

MUD PACK

Chocomint milk shake with a subtle
herbiness.

6 SQUARES OF UNSWEETENED CHOCOLATE

1 PART MILK

1 SCOOP MINT CHOCOLATE CHIP ICE CREAM

GRATED CHOCOLATE

Melt chocolate in milk in a bowl over a pan of
simmering water, or in a microwave on HIGH for
about one minute. Cool. Whiz in a blender with ice
cream to a smooth jungle-green. Pour into a glass
and decorate with grated chocolate. ◼

GHOSTBUSTER

Cool, frothy, creamy and sweet.

4 SQUARES WHITE CHOCOLATE

150ML (2/3 CUP) MILK

2 SCOOPS VANILLA ICE CREAM

Put chocolate and milk in a pan and heat gently until
melted. Cool. Whiz up with ice cream in a blender
for 30 seconds. Serve. ◼

CHAPTER 13

EXOTIC & SPICY

A little touch of luxury never comes amiss.
These drinks include tropical fruits such as
guavas, mangoes and kiwifruit, spices,
coconut and apricots and peaches. Some
are long and refreshing, others are intensely
flavored and served with ice.

CORAL REEF

Luscious strawberry drink with an
intense strawberry scent enhanced by
guava juice.

1 PART GUAVA JUICE

4 STRAWBERRIES, WIPED AND HULLED

STRAWBERRY TO DECORATE

Whiz up all ingredients in a blender for 30 seconds.
Serve with a strawberry on a cocktail stick. ▼

HIGHLAND FLING

2 TBSP TROPICAL FRUIT JUICE

1 PART SPARKLING MINERAL WATER, CHILLED

1 PART BITTER LEMON

Pour fruit juice into a glass. Top up with water and bitter lemon. ▼

TANGO

Neat and colorful juice drink with an interesting raspberry-pink syrup strip on the bottom.

1 PART MANGO JUICE

1 PART ORANGE JUICE

1 TBSP RASPBERRY SYRUP

Mix mango and orange juices. Pour into a glass and carefully drizzle syrup in for a pink layer. ▼

DRACULA'S CLOAK

Deep ruby red. A very sinister cherry drink with a hint of mint.

1 TBSP MINT SYRUP

1 PART CHERRY JUICE

SPRIG OF FRESH MINT

Pour mint syrup into a glass and top up with cherry juice. Decorate with fresh mint. ▼

✳ NIGHT OF PASSION ✳

Pale topaz and sensuously seductive
with a creamy texture and rich taste.

1 PART PASSION FRUIT JUICE

2 TBSP WHIPPING CREAM

1 EGG YOLK

DASH OF ANGOSTURA BITTER

DASH OF SODA WATER

CRUSHED ICE

Shake all ingredients together in a shaker and serve
over crushed ice. ☍

THIRSTY WORK

Refreshing fruity drink flavored with fresh
mango purée and orange and
lemon juice.

100ML (½ CUP) WATER

GRATED RIND OF ½ ORANGE

1 TBSP SUGAR

FLESH OF 1 RIPE MANGO

100ML (½ CUP) ORANGE JUICE

1 TBSP LEMON JUICE

Simmer water, rind and sugar in a pan until sugar
dissolves. Whiz up mango flesh in a blender until
smooth. Add orange and lemon juices and sugar
mix. Chill and serve. ☍

SUGAR AND SPICE

Good drink after a heavy meal.
Makes 1 liter

---

6 TBSP LIGHT BROWN SUGAR

---

2 TBSP GROUND CINNAMON

---

1 TBSP GROUND GINGER

---

1 TSP GROUND CARDAMON

---

1 LITER (5 CUPS) RED GRAPE JUICE

Stir sugar and spices into red grape juice. Leave until spices settle on the bottom. Carefully strain off the clear liquid, leaving dregs behind. Discard. Pour into glasses to serve. 🍷

> It's easier to squeeze more lemon juice if a halved lemon is cooked on HIGH in the microwave for 25 seconds.

TANGO IN THE NIGHT

Butter-yellow and indulgently thick
and fruity.

FLESH OF ½ MANGO

---

1 TBSP CREAM

---

1 PART PINEAPPLE JUICE

**1 TSP BOTTLED SWEETENED
LIME JUICE**

Put all ingredients in a blender and whiz for 30 seconds. Serve. ◼

VANITY FAIR

Spicy cocktail served hot.

300ML (1 ¼ CUPS) MILK

1 VANILLA POD

1 TBSP LIGHT BROWN SUGAR

2 TBSP OATMEAL

PINCH OF CINNAMON TO DECORATE

Put all ingredients in a pan, bring to the boil and simmer until softened. Strain into a heat-resistant glass and sprinkle over cinnamon.

ALMOND GROVE

Nutty, fragrant and citrussy with an attractive chalky lemon color.

1 PART ALMOND SYRUP

1 PART BOTTLED SWEETENED LIME JUICE

TOP UP WITH SPARKLING MINERAL WATER

ICE CUBE FROZEN WITH A WEDGE OF LIME

Pour almond syrup and lime into a glass. Top up with mineral water and serve with a lime ice cube. 🍷

> Pepare plenty of sliced fruit in advance. Cover and chill in the fridge to replenish punch bowls.

SAINT LUCIA

Divine tropical island mix of mango and
papaya, sharpened with lime and
sweetened with honey.

---

1 PAPAYA

---

1 PART MANGO JUICE, CHILLED

JUICE OF ½ LIME

---

2 TBSP HONEY

---

2 ICE CUBES

Peel and halve papaya. Scoop out seeds with a
spoon and roughly chop flesh. Place in a processor
with other ingredients – including ice cubes and whiz
until well blended. Pour into a glass and decorate
with a cocktail umbrella. ▼

★ TREASURE ISLAND ★

Superb fruit drink with sparkling wine,
served in half a melon. Sip this delicious
nectar with melon cupped in both
hands.

---

1 SMALL SWEET MELON

150ML (⅔ CUP) SPARKLING NON-ALCOHOLIC WHITE WINE

150ML (⅔ CUP) APRICOT JUICE

Slice off top third of melon. Scoop melon into a few
balls for decoration. Spoon remaining flesh out
discarding seeds. Purée melon until smooth, mix
with sparkling wine, apricot juice and pour into
melon shell. Thread melon balls onto cocktail stick to
decorate. ▼

WOBBLER

Comforting, fruity, hot and sweet drink.
Don't serve it in the best crystal —
heat-resistant glasses are essential.

---

1 TBSP RED CURRANT JELLY

---

1 PART APPLE JUICE

FEW FRESH MINT LEAVES

FEW WHOLE CLOVES

---

1 CINNAMON STICK

FRESH MINT TO DECORATE

Place all ingredients in a pan and heat gently until
jelly dissolves. Strain into a glass. Decorate with
fresh mint leaves.

FRED AND GINGER

Lovely mix of sweet melon flesh and
spicy ginger ale decorated with green
melon ice cubes.

---

1 MEDIUM HONEYDEW MELON

600ML (2½ CUPS) GINGER ALE

**FEW DROPS OF GREEN VEGETABLE
COLORING**

Cut melon into four and remove seeds. Scoop out
flesh from one quarter using a melon baller. Put
melon balls into ice cube tray. Add water mixed with
green coloring. Freeze. Scoop out remaining flesh
and whiz in a blender until smooth. Pour ginger ale
into a small glass bowl, add melon purée and ice
cubes. Serve. 🍷

TROPICANA

Caribbean delight based on coconut
milk and mango.

FLESH OF ½ MANGO, CHOPPED

---

1 PART COCONUT MILK

COCONUT CURLS, TOASTED TO DECORATE

Whiz mango with milk in a blender until smooth.
Pour into a glass and decorate with toasted coconut
curls. ▼

VICTORIAN LACE

Fragrant, and creamy like cotton lace.

---

1 PART GUAVA JUICE

---

2 SCOOPS VANILLA ICE CREAM

Whiz up in a blender until frothy. Pour into a glass
and decorate with a cocktail umbrella. ▼

AMBER NECTAR

Softly fruity and luxuriously smooth.

---

1 PART APRICOT JUICE

---

1 PART PASSION FRUIT JUICE

---

1 PART SPARKLING MINERAL WATER

ICE CUBES

Mix all ingredients together in a glass. Serve with ice
cubes. ▼

EMERALD

A jewel of a green drink with the delicate
tropical taste of kiwifruit.

---

1 KIWIFRUIT, PEELED AND CHOPPED

---

1 EGG WHITE

---

1 PART APPLE JUICE

---

1 PART SODA WATER

SLICE OF KIWIFRUIT

Whiz kiwifruit and egg white in a blender until frothy
and smooth. Pour into a glass and top up with apple
juice and soda water. Serve in a glass decorated
with a twist of kiwifruit and a green cocktail
stirrer. ￼

EDINBURGH TWIZZLE

Oaty, opaque refresher from Scotland
guaranteed to bring on a chorus of
'Auld Lang Syne'.

---

4 TBSP OATMEAL

---

1 TBSP LIGHT BROWN SUGAR

GRATED RIND AND JUICE OF 1 ORANGE

300ML (1¼ CUPS) BOILING WATER

---

2 THIN SLICES OF ORANGE

Mix oatmeal, sugar, orange rind and juice in a
pitcher. Pour over boiling water and leave to swell.
Chill thoroughly. Strain off the liquid and discard
dregs. Serve and decorate by twisting orange slices
to side of glass. ￼

Thinly slice oranges, lemons and limes.
Freeze until firm and store in polythene bags
in the freezer, ready to use for punch
garnishes.

POOH BEAR

Honey-colored and spicy, cinnamon
and coconut cocktail.

---

1 BANANA, CHOPPED

---

1 TBSP HONEY

150ML (⅔ CUP) COCONUT MILK

PINCH OF GROUND CINNAMON

---

2 ICE CUBES

Put banana, honey, milk and ice cubes in a processor
and whiz until smooth. Pour into a glass and serve
with a straw. ■

PARIS PASSION

Delectable, topaz, perfumed drink with
a sensuous fruit taste.

---

1 PART APRICOT JUICE

---

1 PART PASSION FRUIT JUICE

---

1 PART TONIC WATER

SLICE OF FRESH PEACH

Pour apricot and passion fruit juice into a glass. Top
up with tonic water and decorate· with a peach
slice. ▼

WHITE MISCHIEF

Delicate drink with an oriental fragrance.

FLESH OF 6 LYCHEES

---

1 PART APPLE JUICE

---

1 TSP LIME JUICE

---

1 NASTURTIUM TO DECORATE

Whiz up all ingredients in a blender for 30 seconds.
Float a nasturtium on top to serve. ▼

TARRAGON BEER

Herby long drink with gingery spice.

---

1 TBSP FRESH TARRAGON, CHOPPED

---

2 TBSP BOILING WATER

TOP UP WITH GINGER BEER

Infuse tarragon with water. Cool. Strain into a glass
and top up with ginger beer. ▼

COURT JESTER

Bright-green witty little cocktail.

---

1 TBSP MINT SYRUP

---

1 PART PASSION FRUIT JUICE

---

1 PART SODA WATER

Pour mint syrup into a glass, add passion fruit juice
and top up with soda water. ▼

CHAPTER 14

LOW CALORIE

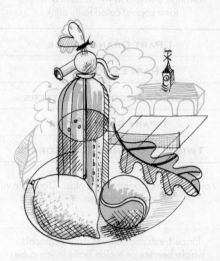

You could just stick to water, it's true as many diet-conscious people do. But for a change try some of these delectable drinks which contain so few calories, it's not worth even adding them up.

STEVENSON'S ROCKET

Pale amber and slightly sparkling bittersweet refresher with a hint of luxury from passion fruit juice.

---

1 PART PASSION FRUIT JUICE

---

1 TSP LEMON JUICE

---

1 PART SODA WATER

Pour passion fruit juice into a glass. Add lemon juice and top up with soda water. 🍷

✳ NOSEY PARKER ✳

Orange and lemon with a dash of bitters
for a sophisticated fruity drink.

---

1 PART ORANGE JUICE

---

1 PART LEMON JUICE

DASH OF ANGOSTURA BITTERS

---

1 PART SODA WATER

TWIST OF ORANGE TO DECORATE

Mix all ingredients together in a glass. Decorate with
an orange twist. ❦

> Place fresh mint leaves, fruit segments,
> whole berries or melon balls in ice cube
> containers, top up with water and freeze
> for fancy ice cubes.

BATTLE OF THE BULGE

Scrumptious strawberry drink for calorie
controlled diets.

300ML (1 ¼ CUPS) LOW FAT SKIMMED MILK

---

8 STRAWBERRIES, HULLED AND WIPED

---

2 TBSP APPLE JUICE

STRAWBERRY TO DECORATE

Whiz up all ingredients in a blender and serve in a
glass decorated with a strawberry on a cocktail
stick. ❦

THIN LIZZY

Fruity yogurt drink with next to no
calories.

150ML (⅔ CUP) LOW FAT PLAIN YOGURT, CHILLED

2 TBSP FRESHLY SQUEEZED ORANGE JUICE

1 EGG

1 TSP ARTIFICIAL SWEETENER

SLICE OF ORANGE

Whiz up all ingredients in a blender and pour into a
glass. Decorate with a slice of orange. ∎

TUTTI FRUTTI

Dainty slivers of garden fruits in
sparkling mineral water.

FLESH OF 1 PEACH, SLICED

2 STRAWBERRIES, HALVED

2 RASPBERRIES

1 SLICE GREEN APPLE

1 PART SPARKLING MINERAL WATER

SLICE OF LIME TO DECORATE

ICE CUBES

Put fruit into a glass. Top up with sparkling mineral
water and decorate with lime slice. Add ice cubes
before serving. 🍸

SLINKY

Apple flavored, low calorie quencher.

150ML (⅔ CUP) SPARKLING MINERAL WATER

150ML (⅔ CUP) UNSWEETENED APPLE JUICE

1 TBSP FRESHLY SQUEEZED LEMON JUICE

FEW APPLE SLICES AND SPRIG OF MINT

Pour water and apple juice into a glass. Stir in lemon juice and add a few apple slices and a sprig of mint for decoration. ▼

SLIM LINE

Think thin yogurt refresher with a pinch of spice.

75ML (⅓ CUP) LOW FAT PLAIN YOGURT, CHILLED

50ML (¼ CUP) GRAPEFRUIT JUICE, CHILLED

1 TSP ARTIFICIAL SWEETENER

PINCH OF GROUND CLOVES

Whiz yogurt, grapefruit juice and sweetener in a blender. Pour into a glass and sprinkle ground cloves on the top. ▼

Check out diet cola, lemonade etc. for reduced calorie cocktails.

Use soda water instead of lemonade to reduce sweetness in fizzy cocktails.

MILORD

Aristocratic and slimming quaff.

150ML (⅔ CUP) FRESHLY MADE WEAK TEA (EARL GREY)

GRATED RIND OF ½ ORANGE

1 TBSP LEMON JUICE

1 TBSP FRESHLY SQUEEZED ORANGE JUICE

FEW ICE CUBES

THIN SLICES OF ORANGE AND LEMON TO DECORATE

Mix tea and orange rind and leave to infuse until cold. Strain into a glass, stir in lemon and orange juice. Serve over ice and decorate with fruit slices. ▼

CHAPTER 15

MILK & YOGURT DRINKS

Somewhat substantial, these milk and yogurt drinks are delicious, sustaining and often thick in texture. Most have a velvety richness and give a memorable and sensuous experience to the palate.

CHEERS

Thick and sultry chocolate and banana cocktail.

4 TBSP FROZEN CHOCOLATE YOGURT

½ BANANA, CHOPPED

1 PART MILK, CHILLED

1 PART LEMONADE

Whiz up all ingredients in a blender. Serve. ▼

BANANA BOAT

Banana treat based on low-fat banana yogurt.

2 TBSP LOW FAT BANANA YOGURT

½ BANANA, CHOPPED

1 TSP MAPLE SYRUP

1 SCOOP VANILLA ICE CREAM

150ML (⅔ CUP) MILK, CHILLED

**PINCH OF GROUND CINNAMON
TO DECORATE**

Whiz up all ingredients in a blender until frothy. Serve decorated with a sprinkling of cinnamon. ▼

★ SHERLOCK HOLMES ★

White, foamy, sweet and sour drink.

1 TBSP BOTTLED SWEETENED LIME JUICE

1 TBSP PLAIN YOGURT

1 TSP HONEY

CRUSHED ICE

DASH OF ANGOSTURA BITTERS

TOP UP WITH LEMONADE

SLICE OF LIME TO DECORATE

Put lime, yogurt and honey in a blender with crushed ice. Whiz up, pour into a glass and add bitters and lemonade. Stir and serve with a slice of lime. ▼

VESUVIUS

Foaming raspberry sherbet.

4 TBSP RASPBERRIES

2 TBSP WHIPPING CREAM

1 EGG WHITE

150ML (2/3 CUP) BITTER LEMON

Whiz up all ingredients in a blender. Pour into a glass and decorate with a cocktail umbrella. ▼

KALAHARI

Interesting and refreshing pale beige drink with a woody scent.

1 PART PRUNE JUICE

1 PART MILK, CHILLED

Mix prune juice and milk together in a glass and serve. 🍷

CHERRY SOUR

Pale mauve and refreshing cherry sour which stimulates the taste buds.

1 PART CHERRY JUICE

1 PART MILK, CHILLED

FRESH CHERRY TO DECORATE

Pour cherry juice into a glass, top up with milk and decorate with a cherry. 🍷

YOGI BEAR

Thick and fruity, with a hint of pink. Serve
ice cold.

150ML (⅔ CUP) STRAWBERRY YOGURT

½ BANANA, CHOPPED

---

1 TBSP HONEY

---

1 LARGE SCOOP VANILLA ICE CREAM

SLICE OF BANANA

Place all ingredients in a blender except for banana
slice, and blend until smooth. Serve in a chilled glass
and top with a banana slice. ▼

> Don't own a processor? – blend cocktail in a
> bowl with a hand mixer. Crush ice by
> wrapping in a clean tea towel and hitting
> with a rolling pin.

BLUEBERRY HILL

Pale mauve milk and yogurt drink
with the refreshing tang of blueberry
juice.

---

2 TBSP CANNED BLUEBERRIES

---

1 TBSP BLUEBERRY JUICE

---

1 PART MILK, CHILLED

---

1 TBSP THICK YOGURT

Whiz up all the ingredients in a blender until smooth.
Serve. ▼

CHIMPERS

Creamy, thick and satisfying drink
based on plain yogurt. Use a low fat
yogurt for a lower calorie count.

---

1 BANANA, CHOPPED

150ML (⅔ CUP) PINEAPPLE JUICE

---

1 EGG, BEATEN

---

1 TBSP PLAIN YOGURT

WHOLE CHERRY TO DECORATE

Put banana, pineapple juice, egg and yogurt in a
blender and whiz until smooth. Chill. Pour into a
glass and serve with a cherry. ■

LITTLE JACK HORNER

Baby-pink, creamy and frothy with a
slightly sour plum freshness.

FLESH OF 1 RIPE RED PLUM

---

1 PART BUTTERMILK

---

1 PART VANILLA ICE CREAM

Remove skin from plum, halve and place in
a blender with buttermilk and vanilla ice cream.
Whiz up until smooth. Serve. ▼

Suit the glass to the cocktail: tall tumblers for
thirst quenching fizzes; short, chunky glasses
for thick, creamy, or rich tasting drinks;
cocktail glasses for exotic delicacies;
wineglasses for fruit mixtures.

EGGNOGGIN PLUS

Delicious, light, and nutritious too.

300ML (1¼ CUPS) MILK, CHILLED

---

1 EGG

¼ TSP VANILLA EXTRACT

---

2 TBSP SUGAR

PINCH OF GROUND NUTMEG TO DECORATE

Mix all ingredients, except nutmeg, in a blender at high speed until frothy. Pour into a glass and sprinkle with ground nutmeg. ♟

COCONUT PARADISE

Pretty two-tone, pale pink fading into white on top and subtly flavored with coconut.

---

2 PARTS MILK

---

1 TBSP DRIED COCONUT

---

2 TBSP STRAWBERRY SYRUP

---

1 TBSP STRAWBERRY SYRUP AND 1 TBSP DRIED COCONUT FOR RIM

Heat milk gently with coconut to infuse with a delicate taste. Leave until milk cools then strain into a pitcher. Chill. Dip rim of a tall glass into strawberry syrup, then into remainder of coconut. Carefully spoon syrup into a glass, then top up with chilled infused milk. ♟

SHIPWRECK

Smooth, thick and creamy banana whiz.

---

1 RIPE BANANA, PEELED AND CUT
INTO CHUNKS

DASH OF LEMON JUICE

---

1 TBSP LIGHT BROWN SUGAR

---

1 PART WHIPPING CREAM

---

1 PART MILK, CHILLED

GRATED CHOCOLATE
TO DECORATE

Put banana and lemon juice in a blender and whiz
until smooth. Add sugar, cream and milk and blend
until light and frothy. Serve in a glass with grated
chocolate on the top. ◼

THE WALDORF

Smooth, coffee and banana drink
topped with walnuts.

---

1 RIPE BANANA, CHOPPED

JUICE OF ½ LEMON

150ML (⅔ CUP) MILK, CHILLED

---

1 TBSP COFFEE EXTRACT

---

1 TSP WALNUTS, FINELY CHOPPED TO
DECORATE

Blend together banana, lemon juice, milk, coffee
extract and crushed ice in a blender. Pour into a
glass and sprinkle over walnuts to serve. 🍷

JET LAG

Pale pink, raspberry and honey milk
drink.

---

4 TBSP RASPBERRIES

---

1 PART MILK, CHILLED

---

1 TBSP HONEY

---

1 ICE CUBE

**FRESH RASPBERRIES AND LEAVES
TO DECORATE**

Purée raspberries and strain to remove seeds. Whiz
purée in a processor with milk, honey and ice for 30
seconds. Pour into a glass and decorate with fresh
raspberries and a few leaves. ▼

FATAL ATTRACTION

Thick and fruity yogurt drink, made with
fresh strawberries.

**4 TBSP STRAWBERRIES, WIPED AND
HULLED**

---

1 TBSP HONEY

150ML (⅔ CUP) PLAIN YOGURT

ICE CUBES

**WHOLE STRAWBERRY DIPPED IN
SUPERFINE SUGAR TO DECORATE**

Whiz up strawberries in a processor until smooth. Add
honey, yogurt, ice and blend thoroughly. Pour into a
glass and secure strawberry to rim with a cocktail
stick. ▼

Dilute yogurt with milk for a smoother taste.
Low fat yogurt can be used if preferred.

NECTAR OF THE GODS

Creamy, thick and almond scented drink
with a velvety richness.

---

1 TBSP LEMON JUICE

---

1 TBSP GROUND ALMONDS

---

2 TBSP ALMOND SYRUP

300ML (1 ¼ CUPS) MILK, CHILLED

Pour lemon juice onto a flat saucer and place glass
upside down to wet rim. Then dip in a saucer of
ground almonds for a delicate almond edge. Pour
syrup into glass and add milk, without disturbing
almond rim, then stir. ■

SCORCHER

Cooling and very pretty buttermilk drink,
tasting of raspberries.

150ML (⅔ CUP) BUTTERMILK, CHILLED

---

2 TBSP RASPBERRIES

---

2 ICE CUBES

---

1 EGG WHITE

FEW FRESH RASPBERRIES TO DECORATE

Blend first four ingredients until frothy in a processor.
Serve chilled, decorated with whole fresh raspberries. ■

LATE NIGHT MOVIE

Mauve, marble effect on bottom of
glass through to a subtle black currant
color.

½ PART BLACK CURRANT SYRUP

1 PART MILK, CHILLED

1 LARGE SCOOP VANILLA ICE CREAM

2 WHOLE HAZELNUTS, FINELY CHOPPED

BLACK CURRANT SYRUP TO DECORATE

Pour black currant syrup into a glass. Add milk and
a large scoop of ice cream. Sprinkle over nuts and a
drizzle of black currant syrup. ◼

NUTCASE

Substantial snack drink – but deliciously
refreshing all the same.

150ML (⅔ CUP) SOYA MILK

150ML (⅔ CUP) MILK

4 SQUARES UNSWEETENED CHOCOLATE

3 TBSP PLAIN YOGURT

1 TBSP SUGAR

1 TBSP HAZELNUTS, CHOPPED

Pour both milks into a pan with chocolate and heat
gently until chocolate melts. Stir to mix. Cover and
cool. Spoon in yogurt, sugar and hazelnuts and whiz
up in a blender until it's a pale nutty color. Serve. 🍸

BUBBLES

Peppermint-green, smooth and thick minty drink, topped with opaque jade bubbles. Delicious for after dinner. Serve in a glass with the rim frosted with green sugar.

1 TBSP GREEN MINT SYRUP AND 1 TSP SUGAR FOR RIM

1 PART MINT SYRUP

2 PARTS LIGHT CREAM

2 ICE CUBES

FEW FRESH MINT LEAVES

Dip rim of glass in mint syrup then in sugar for a green frosty edge. Mix syrup and cream to a smooth green. Put ice cubes in a processor and whiz for six seconds to crush. Pour mint mix over ice and serve in a glass decorated with mint leaves.

GEEWHIZZ

Pale mauve and marbled, sweet maple syrup drink.

2 TBSP BLACKBERRIES

1 TBSP MAPLE SYRUP

2 TBSP THICK PLAIN YOGURT

150ML (2/3 CUP) LEMONADE

Blend blackberries and maple syrup in a blender until smooth. Pour into a glass and stir in yogurt for a marbled effect. Top up with lemonade and chill before serving.

TEDDY BOY

Creamy yogurt drink with apricots.

---

1 PART APRICOT JUICE

1 TBSP PLAIN YOGURT

1 PART LEMONADE

Combine all ingredients in a blender until frothy and serve. 🍸

LADY PENELOPE

Frothy, cadillac-pink yogurt drink.

---

1 PART STRAWBERRY SYRUP

1 EGG WHITE

1 PART PLAIN YOGURT, CHILLED

Put all ingredients into a bowl and whiz up with a mixer until bubbles form and it looks light and frothy. Pour into a glass and serve immediately. 🍶

PINBALL WIZARD

Carmine-pink, thick buttermilk refresher.

---

1 PART FRESH RED CURRANTS

1 PART BUTTERMILK, CHILLED

1 PART RASPBERRY RIPPLE ICE CREAM

Remove stalks from red currants, wash and dry well. Place in a blender with buttermilk and ice cream. Pour into a glass and serve with a straw. 🍸

EGGNOGGIN

Rich, thick and frothy eggnog.

---

2 TBSP HONEY

---

1 EGG

150ML (⅔ CUP) MILK, CHILLED

PINCH OF GROUND CINNAMON

Beat honey and egg together until thick and frothy. Beat in milk, pour into a glass and sprinkle ground cinnamon on top. 🍷

For a large party buy ice cubes in bulk.

FAT HARRY

A definite taste of the east in this delicious white drink.

300ML (1 ¼ CUPS) MILK

---

1 CINNAMON STICK

---

2 TSP GROUND ALMONDS

---

1 TSP ROSE WATER

---

1 TSP GRATED LEMON RIND

---

1 TBSP SOFT BROWN SUGAR

Place all ingredients in a pan. Bring to the boil, remove from heat and leave until cold. Strain into a glass and chill before serving. 🍸

CHAPTER 16

CRUSHED ICE

The latest refreshing slushes. Drinks based on crushed ice, flavored with fresh fruits and syrup and drunk through a fat straw as the ice begins to melt.

GOLD DIGGER

Fresh orange slush spiked with lemon.

FRESHLY SQUEEZED JUICE OF 3 ORANGES

---

4 TBSP MINERAL WATER

---

1 TBSP LEMON JUICE

Mix juices with mineral water and pour into a freezer proof container. Freeze until firm and break up with a fork. Scoop into a glass to serve. ▼

TOADY

Delicate pale green slush with lime.

6 TBSP BOTTLED SWEETENED LIME JUICE

300ML (1 ¼ CUPS) MINERAL WATER

Mix lime juice and water. Pour into a freezer proof container. Freeze until firm and break up with a fork. Scoop into a glass to serve. ▼

SUPER SCOOP

Refreshing slush with a sherbety base.

2 SCOOPS ORANGE SORBET (SHERBET)

2 SCOOPS CRUSHED ICE

1 TBSP ALMOND SYRUP

Mash sorbet with ice. Spoon into a glass and drizzle almond syrup on top to serve. Drink through a straw as ice melts. ▼

SLEDGEHAMMER

2 SCOOPS LEMON SORBET (SHERBET)

2 SCOOPS CRUSHED ICE

1 TBSP STRAWBERRY SYRUP

Mash sorbet with ice. Spoon into a glass and drizzle strawberry syrup on top to serve. Drink through a straw as ice melts. ▪

MIDNIGHT EXPRESS

Black currant slush for a healthy
refresher.

2 SCOOPS BLACK CURRANT SORBET (SHERBET)

1 SCOOP CRUSHED ICE

DASH OF LEMON JUICE

SQUIRT OF SODA

Mash sorbet with ice and lemon juice. Spoon into a
glass and add a squirt of soda to taste. ▼

> Crush ice by
> wrapping in a clean towel and hitting
> with a rolling pin

SLUSHES

To make one slush whiz up 10 ice cubes
in a processor. Top up with any *one* of the
following or dream up your own!

3 TBSP STRAWBERRY SYRUP

150ML (2/3 CUP) PINEAPPLE JUICE

150ML (2/3 CUP) MANGO JUICE

3 TBSP BOTTLED SWEETENED LIME JUICE

3 TBSP BLACK CURRANT SYRUP

Pour into a glass and drink through a straw as the
ice melts. ▼

KIWI SLUSH

Green and speckly crushed ice drink.

2 KIWIFRUIT, PEELED AND PURÉED

1 TBSP HONEY

150ML (⅔ CUP) MINERAL WATER

SLICE OF KIWIFRUIT TO DECORATE

Mix kiwifruit with honey and water. Pour into a container and freeze until firm. Break up with a fork and scoop into a glass. Decorate with kiwifruit slice. ☂

OUTER SPACE

Citrussy slush with a hint of mint and served in a grapefruit shell.

1 GRAPEFRUIT, TOP THIRD REMOVED

2 SCOOPS LEMON SORBET (SHERBET)

1 TSP MINT SYRUP

Scoop flesh from grapefruit to leave a clean pith-free shell. Whiz flesh in a blender then strain juice into a pitcher. Mash in sorbet and syrup and spoon into a grapefruit shell. Drink through a straw. ■

CHAPTER 17

PARTY PUNCHES

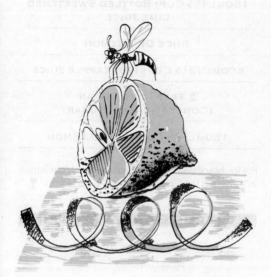

Having a party? There is something for everybody in this bunch of punches, providing alcohol-free, fun drinks for non-drinkers, drivers and the children. Drink them on picnics — they travel well in flasks — at barbecues or in the garden. They're festive and colorful and a world away from boring old fruit cups.

SPLASH

Delicate summer punch. Makes 1 liter

ICE BLOCK

150ML (⅔ CUP) BOTTLED SWEETENED LIME JUICE

JUICE OF 1 LEMON

600ML (2½ CUPS) PINEAPPLE JUICE

2 TBSP ICING SUGAR (CONFECTIONERS' SUGAR)

150ML (⅔ CUP) BITTER LEMON

Put ice block and all ingredients except bitter lemon in bowl and stir. Chill and top with bitter lemon. 🍸

CITRUS BARLEY WATER

Deliciously cooling refresher for tennis players. Makes 1 liter

6 TBSP PEARL BARLEY, WASHED

2 LARGE JUICY LEMONS, WASHED

1 LITER (5 CUPS) BOILING WATER

2 TBSP CUBE SUGAR

Place barley in a large pan and cover with cold water. Bring to the boil and simmer for four minutes. Strain. Transfer to a pitcher. Thinly pare rind from lemons and add to barley. Pour over boiling water, add sugar and stir until dissolved. Cool and squeeze over juice from lemons, stirring to mix. Strain and chill well before serving in a tall pitcher decorated with lemon twists. 🍸

THE GRAPE ESCAPE

Stimulating drink, garnished with grapes
and cherries and chilled with mint ice
cubes. Makes 3 liters

---

1 ¼ LITERS (6 CUPS) SPARKLING RED
GRAPE JUICE

---

1 ¼ LITERS (6 CUPS) CHERRY JUICE

½ LITER (2 ¼ CUPS) GRAPEFRUIT JUICE

WHOLE CHERRIES, WASHED
AND PITTED

SEEDLESS GRAPES

FRESH MINT LEAVES FROZEN IN
ICE CUBES

Mix juices together in a large bowl. Add fruit and ice
cubes just before serving. 🍷

★ MELODRAMATIC PUNCH ★

Red punch served in a scooped out
watermelon. Cut a thin slice off the
bottom to make sure it doesn't topple
over. Makes 1 liter

---

1 MEDIUM SIZED WATERMELON, TOP
THIRD REMOVED

600ML (2 ½ CUPS) SPARKLING RED
GRAPE JUICE

300ML (1 ¼ CUPS) ORANGE JUICE

---

2 TBSP BLACK CURRANT SYRUP

Scoop out a few melon balls for decoration,

discarding seeds. Hollow out remaining flesh and remove seeds, retaining any juice. Purée melon flesh with juice in a blender. Pour into melon shell, add grape and orange juices and black currant syrup. Don't overfill. Stir. Serve with melon balls floating on the top. ♟

> For a cool punch, add a block of ice. Make by freezing water in the ice cube container with the grid removed. A block takes longer to thaw than ice cubes.

CRAZY CUP

Fun, fresh and fruity. The kind of drink
which makes you smile!
Makes 1 liter

---

1 FRESH PINEAPPLE

FEW COCKTAIL CHERRIES

**1 ORANGE, SKIN WIPED AND CUT
INTO WEDGES**

**1 RED SKINNED APPLE, CORED AND
CUT INTO CHUNKS**

---

3 TBSP LIGHT BROWN SUGAR

½ LITER (2½ CUPS) GINGER BEER

½ LITER (2½ CUPS) LEMONADE

ICE CUBES TO SERVE

Pare skin from pineapple and cut flesh into chunks. Place in a large punch bowl with rest of the fruit. Stir in sugar and leave to stand for two hours. Add ginger beer, lemonade and lots of ice. Ladle into glasses to serve. ♟

ICEBREAKER

Fresh fruit and mint tea punch.
Makes 1 liter

---

4 TEA BAGS

600ML (2½ CUPS) BOILING WATER

---

2 TBSP SUGAR

425ML (2 CUPS) ORANGE JUICE

---

1 ORANGE, SLICED

---

1 LEMON, SLICED

FEW MINT LEAVES TO DECORATE

**ICE CUBES FROZEN WITH WHOLE
HULLED STRAWBERRIES**

Infuse tea bags in water for two minutes. Strain liquid into punch bowl, add sugar and stir to dissolve. Pour in orange juice, add fruit and cool. Decorate with mint and strawberry ice cubes. 🍷

SPICED ALE PUNCH

A heavenly, warm and spicy punch,
ideal for chilly winter evenings.
Makes 1½ liters

---

1 LITER (5 CUPS) GINGER ALE

---

4 WHOLE CLOVES

PINCH OF MIXED SPICE

½ TSP GROUND NUTMEG

---

1 TBSP SUGAR

---

2 DESSERT APPLES, CORED AND CHOPPED

WEDGE OF APPLE TO DECORATE

Gently heat ginger ale with cloves, spice and sugar for three minutes. Add apple, remove from heat and leave to infuse for ten minutes. Strain into a pitcher, then pour into glasses. Serve with a wedge of apple floating on top. ♟

★ COUNTRY GARDEN ★

Delightful and delicately fresh herbal brew with raspberries and topped with grape and pineapple juices for a divine refresher. Makes 1 liter

LARGE BUNCH OF FRESH MINT

BUNCH OF LEMON BALM

300ML (1 ¼ CUPS) WATER

2 TBSP RASPBERRIES

1 ORANGE

1 LEMON

300ML (1 ¼ CUPS) WHITE GRAPE JUICE

300ML (1 ¼ CUPS) PINEAPPLE JUICE

SPRIG OF FRESH ROSEMARY

Whiz up mint, lemon balm, water and raspberries in a blender for 30 seconds. Grate rind from orange and lemon, add rind and freshly squeezed juice to mix. Leave to soak for 15 minutes. Strain into a pitcher and top up with grape and pineapple juices. Chill and decorate with rosemary sprigs. ♟

★ SHAMGRIA ★

Non-alcoholic version of Spain's
favorite punch.
Makes 1 liter

**1 BOTTLE NON-ALCOHOLIC DRY
RED WINE**

---

3 TBSP SUGAR

---

1 PART ORANGE JUICE

---

2 ORANGES, SLICED

---

2 APPLES, CORED AND SLICED

---

2 LIMES, SLICED

**TOP UP WITH LEMONADE,
CHILLED**

Mix all wine, sugar, orange juice and half the fruit in a large bowl. Cover and leave overnight. Strain and discard fruit, replacing it with remaining unused fruit. Top up with lemonade before serving in a glass pitcher. ▼

SHAKESPEARE PUNCH

Amber punch made with tea and
flavored with dried fruit.
Makes 2½ liters

**3 TBSP DRIED PRUNES, PITTED
AND FINELY CHOPPED**

**3 TBSP DRIED DATES, PITTED
AND FINELY CHOPPED**

**3 TBSP DRIED APRICOTS, FINELY
CHOPPED**

---

1 ¼ LITERS (6 CUPS) FRESHLY MADE
EARL GREY TEA

1 ¼ LITERS (6 CUPS) ORANGE JUICE

1 ORANGE, SLICED

Poach dried fruit in the tea until it softens. Strain into
a large bowl. Chill and add orange juice and slices
of fruit. 🍸

★ HONEYSUCKLE PUNCH ★

Pretty non-alcoholic white wine punch,
decorated with colorful fruit.
Makes 2 liters

1 BOTTLE NON-ALCOHOLIC DRY WHITE
WINE, CHILLED

2 TBSP HONEY

1 STAR FRUIT, SLICED

FLESH OF 1 PEACH, SLICED

FEW FRESH CHERRIES, HALVED
AND PITTED

1 LITER (5 CUPS) LEMONADE, CHILLED

ICE CUBES FROZEN WITH HONEYSUCKLE
FLOWERS

Mix wine, honey and fruit in a large glass bowl.
Cover and leave in a cool place for one hour. Add
lemonade and serve with honeysuckle ice cubes. 🍸

INDEX OF INGREDIENTS